747 BUDGET
BUDGET LIVING :HOME
CHEAP HOME : A ROOM BY
WITHDRAWN

BUDGET LIVING

Home Cheap Home

A ROOM-BY-ROOM GUIDE TO GREAT DECORATING

500 Ideas

From the Editors of *Budget Living* Magazine

A PERIGEE BOOK

ALAMEDA FREE LIBRARY
2200-A Central Avenue
Alameda, CA 94501

A Perigee Book
Published by The Berkley Publishing Group
A division of Penguin Group (USA) Inc.
375 Hudson Street
New York, New York 10014

Copyright © 2004 by Budget Living LLC

Book design by Toby Fox
Cover design by Toby Fox and Ben Gibson
Icon illustrations by Jason Schneider

Editing by Kathleen Hackett

All rights reserved. This book, or parts thereof, may not be reproduced in any form without permission. The scanning, uploading, and distribution of this book via the Internet or via any other means without the permission of the publisher is illegal and punishable by law. Please purchase only authorized electronic editions, and do not participate in or encourage electronic piracy of copyrighted materials. Your support of the author's rights is appreciated.

The photograph and illustration credits which appear on page 189 are incorporated herein by reference.

Perigee trade paperback edition: May 2004

Visit our website at www.penguin.com.

This book has been cataloged by the Library of Congress.

Printed in the United States of America
10 9 8 7 6 5 4 3 2 1

Budget Living Magazine
317 Madison Avenue, Suite 2300
New York, New York 10017
212-687-6060; fax: 212-687-5222

Budget Living magazine is published bimonthly. Subscription prices, payable in U.S. funds, are $19.95 for one year (six issues). Additional postage: In Canada, add $10, and in all other foreign countries, add $15 per year. To subscribe or renew: Call 800-588-1644 or visit www.BudgetLivingMedia.com.

Budget Living, *Spend Smart. Live Rich.*, *Home Cheap Home*, and *Party Central* are trademarks of Budget Living LLC.

Acknowledgments

AT BUDGET LIVING, WE BELIEVE that the things you make yourself are always more meaningful than pricey purchased products—and we practice what we preach. That's why a tiny band of us insists on creating the magazine without an expensive entourage of stylists, producers, location scouts, lunch getters, and second-guessers. So when we decided to publish a book, the same small staff got involved—especially Alex Bhattacharji, Gregory Garry, Sheri Geller, Winnie Lee, Rose Reis, and John Voelcker. But even the most hard-core D.I.Y. types need professional help sometimes (and not just of the psychiatric variety). *Home Cheap Home* wouldn't exist without the indispensable freelancers we're lucky enough to call friends. Art director Toby Fox and editor-writer Kathleen Hackett steered this project from the very beginning, while Michael Boodro (once again) came to my rescue at the end. The marvelous Meg Matyia pitched in on the photo side; research editor Matthew Schuerman was responsible for the facts; and copy editors Bob Bowe, Danielle Dowling, and Marie Timell kept us in line grammarwise.

The same photographers and writers who give the magazine its look and voice also contributed to these pages. The photographers are listed on page 189; the writers are Alison Alfandre, Michael Boodro, Laura Fenton, Kathleen Hackett, Susan Heeger, Christy Hobart, Winnie Lee, Julie Mihaly, Lynne Palazzi, Rose Reis, Kathleen Renda, Diane Dorrans Saeks, Jessica Strand, Constance Van Flandern, Laura J. Vogel, Natalie Warady, Catherine Whalen, and Caroline Whitbeck. Providing them with material were the daring yet down-to-earth designers, architects, and home owners who opened their doors to us: Demi Adeniran; Brenda, John, and Stephen Atkinson; Russ Cletta; Rebecca Cole; Christopher Coleman; Chip Cordelli; Chantal Dussouchaud and Harry Dolman; Sasha Emerson and Larry Levin; Elaine Gemmell; Genifer Goodman and Benjamin Sohr; Nick Grad and Carolyn Bernstein; Andy Hackman; Allen and Paulette Hoggatt; Jolie Kelter and Michael Malcé; Jean Klebs; Mary Catherine Lamb; Charles de Lisle; Henry Mitchell; Laurie and Brian Murphy; Mark Naden; Lynne Palazzi and Chris Raymond; Rob Pruitt and Jonathan Horowitz; Darren Ransdell; Liza Schoenfein and Mark Jannot; and Lauri Ward.

Of course, not a single page of *Home Cheap Home* would have been printed without our professional (and extremely patient) production team: Michael Breen of Spectragraphic, and Janet Mannheimer and Ellen Marin of the aptly named Publishing Experts. A special thanks to Michelle Howry and John Duff of Perigee/Penguin for teaching us Budgeteers what book publishing is all about. And finally, Don Welsh and Eric Rayman: I don't know what possessed you to entrust your publishing company to a smart-aleck whippersnapper like myself, but I sure am glad you did.

—SARAH GRAY MILLER, Editor-in-Chief, *Budget Living*

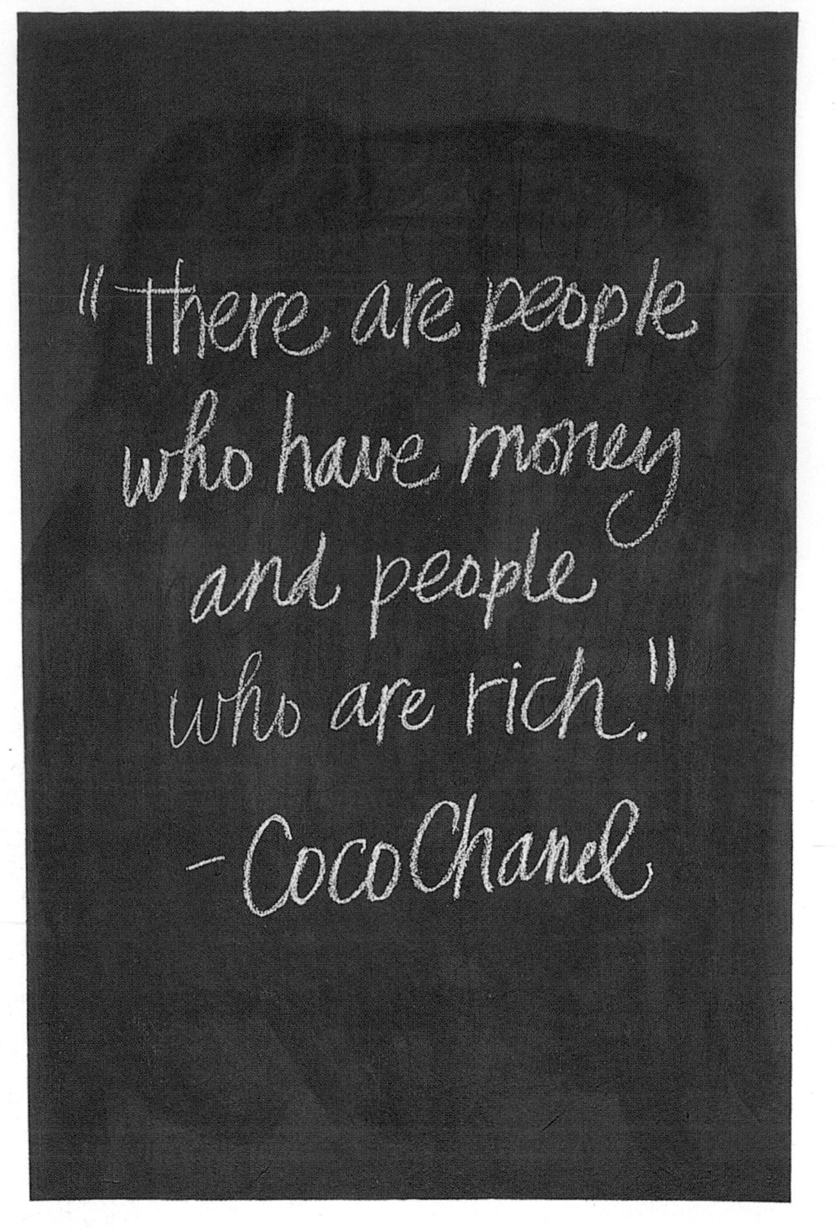
"There are people
who have money
and people
who are rich."
-Coco Chanel

Downhome
My Mississippi
THE GARDEN BOOK
DAVE EGGERS
GARDEN
Seaside Interiors
ALPHABETS

Contents

Introduction

Few things strike as much fear into people's hearts as the prospect of decorating. Even fashionable types, who effortlessly pull together outfits and treat thrift shops like designer boutiques, freeze up when faced with having to buy a new sofa or select tile for the kitchen. And that's before the inevitable sticker shock sets in. At *Budget Living*, we've always believed that style is a matter of attitude, not price. To demystify design, we've turned to professionals–decorators, architects, and stylists–not to show the elaborate projects they tackle for wealthy clients, but to uncover how they live on their own time (and dimes). Their budgets probably aren't much bigger than yours, but they have knowledge and access to resources that you haven't had–until now. More important, these experts are confident enough to see their homes as an outlet for personal expression. Our hope is that you find inspiration in their fearless approach and learn from their example how to put your own unique stamp on your space. So we've culled the best insider ideas from the magazine's pages–and added a bunch of new ones–to create this room-by-room decorating guide. It's 192 pages of proof that you *can* live the good life on the cheap. Whether you're an accomplished aesthete or wouldn't know an Eames from an emu, whether you have 500 square feet or five children underfoot, the building blocks for creating a beautiful space on a budget are the same.

Expensive modern art? Nah. The large abstract image on Benjamin Sohr's mantel, opposite, was scribbled by his four-year-old daughter, Lucy.

GIRL SCOUTS
HAVE FUN
GS

Think, don't spend: Get over the idea that dropping big bucks is the solution. Use your head instead of your wallet. The following pages are filled with clever concepts that will get your brain in gear. **Give class to mass:** Go ahead and shop at the big chain stores. Just make sure your house doesn't wind up looking like a catalog for one. We'll show you how to take what you buy–from Ikea cabinets to Bed Bath & Beyond linens to Crate and Barrel glassware–and make it your own. **Break boundaries:** Bring outdoor furniture inside, use a fish trap as a lamp shade, create a border out of vintage handkerchiefs. Refuse to be limited by what someone else says is appropriate. Just because it isn't done doesn't mean you shouldn't do it. **Use your hands:** You needn't be a professional to paint, install shelves, or build a simple outdoor deck. We'll give you direction–and also tell you when the smartest move is to hire an expert. **Splurge:** As important as knowing how to save is knowing when to fork over a few dollars. The idea is not to feel deprived, but to use your money well. Sometimes that big expensive gesture is just what a room needs. **Laugh:** One benefit to buying inexpensive furnishings is that you don't have to take them so darn seriously. The less you spend, the freer you'll feel to experiment until you've created a home that truly expresses who you are and what you love. Have a little fun. Relax–this isn't brain surgery; it's only your living room.

A great lineup: In Mary Catherine Lamb's bedroom, opposite, vintage handkerchiefs become a witty substitute for a wallpaper border.

1

Should you cart home that cast-off couch? Splurge on a chandelier? Reconsider your coffee table? We've got the affordable answers for making your living room a better place to, well, live.

Living Rooms

Sick of socking it away for a couch you can't really swing? Not to mention a carpet that costs a pile? For less than the price of a mini vacation, you can make your living room a place you can't wait to kick back in. Sound impossible? Just try some of the decorating tips from the tightwads in this chapter. There's a designer who turned a tiny box into a deceptively spacious living room with cheap mirrors, Salvation Army cast-offs, and a gallon of paint; two artists who didn't spend more than $500 on any one piece of furniture; a couple who cleverly combined their clashing styles by mixing masculine furnishings with feminine fabrics; and a collector who cares as much for Matchbox cars as he does for rare Swedish glass. If the cheapskate in you can't see spending one thin dime on decorating, there's hope for you, too. Check out the living room redo that shows you how to make your pad more pleasant using stuff you already own. ✻ If you're dying for a D.I.Y. project to give your living room a lift, copy one of the coffee table makeovers, compliments of four funky designers, give a stained chair a perky patch job, and paper your city apartment walls with, say, a view of snowcapped mountains and a white-tailed deer or two. Or carve a zebra-shaped carpet from leftover flooring. Whichever way you slice it, you won't spend an arm and a leg to breathe a little (wild) life into your living room.

1
2
3
4
5
6

YOU CAN LIVE LARGE IN A TINY LIVING ROOM ON THE CHEAP.

The Space Case

WHEN INTERIOR designer Demi Adeniran had the opportunity to buy the top floor of the Brooklyn town house where she had been living, she leaped at the chance. Never mind that the small one-bedroom apartment was in less-than-perfect shape. Only an optimist like Adeniran could have transformed the dark, cramped living room into an open, airy space that seems deceptively large—especially considering the diminutive size of this decorator's budget. How did she pull it off? By refurbishing Salvation Army cast-offs and relying on mirrors (not a costly architectural addition) to create the illusion of extra square footage. But while saving money was integral to Adeniran's success, so was her willingness to spend when necessary. Her splurges included a $1,200 Murano glass chandelier and a cast-iron fireplace.

Demi Adeniran serves up a martini at the bar cart she found in a Salvation Army thrift shop.

Small Wonder

Adeniran's living room may feel airy and expansive, but the entire area measures a scant 290 square feet, about one-half of her entire apartment. The designer's secrets?

1 A BALANCED VIEW Symmetry is essential when space is limited. To prevent visual confusion in the living room, Adeniran "doubled" the single window on one side of the fireplace with a set of Ikea shelves on the other.

2 COLOR CODE For once, conventional wisdom is correct: White walls do make a small place seem larger, but that doesn't mean you can't have a little fun. Adeniran kept her bold choice of chartreuse paint confined to the entryway and one living room wall.

3 VISUAL TRICKERY Mirrors, propped and hung everywhere, create the illusion of more room. Their reflective surfaces also bounce light throughout the apartment, attracting the eye and averting boredom.

4 A SIMPLE PLAN The designer knew that elaborate window treatments would overwhelm the tiny living room, so she opted for simple sheer shades that recede into the wall while letting the sun shine in.

5 SEATING ARRANGEMENTS Adeniran loves to entertain, but she didn't want to crowd her cramped apartment with chairs. The solution: movable (and affordable) floor cushions that provide guests with plenty of places to sit without eating up a bit of vertical space.

6 SCREEN SAVER Even in a small room, high ceilings can make the furniture seem like it's floating. Adeniran anchored one corner with a Moorish wrought iron screen that does more than just stand there. The openwork panels add dimension and texture to the gap between the wall and the chair—creating a feeling of coziness without adding clutter.

Got a tiny place? A tight budget? You can still make room for big-time glamour if you follow Adeniran's principles.

Obey the Urge to Splurge

Just as a pricey handbag can dress up a white T-shirt, one luxurious decorative detail has the power to elevate every object that basks in its glow. That's why Adeniran spent more on her Murano chandelier—$1,200—than on any other item in her living room. How do you decide what to splurge on? Answer one question honestly, and it's a no-brainer: Does the piece add the kind of quirky impact that defines your personal style?

Choose the Right White

"I lived with a lot of color before," Adeniran says of her previous apartment, "but I find white more serene." The challenge: choosing the right shade among those endless swatches at the paint store. Go too white and your walls will have a droning institutional glow. Not white enough and they'll look dingy. That's why Adeniran swears by Benjamin Moore Regal Wall Satin Flat Finish in Decorator's White. It's the only white your walls should ever know. It gives a clean-looking finish that's not jarring and free of any weird bluish or yellowish tint.

Collect Without Cluttering

Adeniran proves that a mad collector can achieve a minimalist look in a tiny apartment. The key is to resist the temptation to pick up every shiny bauble that catches your eye. You have to set boundaries—even if one of them is as loose as color. Adeniran collects all things orange (including these vases, chopsticks, and salt and pepper shakers, above), as well as masks and mercury glass. She gets away with it by grouping like objects together to make one strong visual statement.

PROJECT:
REFLECT ON THIS

You don't have to share Adeniran's passion for picking up hard-to-find mercury glass to make your living room shelves look like you've been plying the aisles of flea markets for years. These homemade beauties may not fetch the hundreds of dollars that the real stuff can command, but they will give your room a similarly dusky glow. The cost: around $12 for Krylon's Looking Glass Mirror-Like Two Step Kit. Simply spritz five light coats of the base paint on the inside or underside of any clear glass object: a ho-hum florist's vase, a cheap plate from a 99-cent store, even a fishbowl. Then wait 15 minutes and spray on a single layer of a clear protective coat to prevent scratching or chipping. The experts at Krylon suggest cleaning the glass thoroughly before painting it, but if you leave the vases a tad on the funky side, you'll get a more imperfect vintage look. The results? Three shining examples of they'll-never-know-the-difference chic.

Yes, you can put two couches in a cozy living room. Rob Pruitt and Jonathan Horowitz bartered a modern sofa for this pair of pleather pieces.

The Dark Side

ANYONE ELSE would have been scared off by the piles of mismatched bric-a-brac and aged floral wallpaper. But amid a decaying Victorian mansion in the Catskills, artists Rob Pruitt and Jonathan Horowitz saw the makings of a living room that could stop people dead. One and a half years later, with dark humor and daring decorating choices, they forged a live-in installation that highlights their respective talents—painting and conceptual art. The brooding space is brimming with so many affordable visual tricks and treats and doable decorating ideas, it's frightening. And through it all, the self-described cheapskates stayed in the black. How? They haunted a local auction house, bid like demons on eBay, used plenty of elbow grease, and followed one rule: No piece could cost more than $500.

Exquisite Noir

They say the devil is in the details, but in this living room, the wickedness is pure Pruitt and Horowitz. "We're much more excited by cinematic, skin-deep fakery than tasteful decor," says Pruitt. Their sinister style secrets?

DESIGNER DECEPTIONS Painted "moldings" killed all the right angles in the room. By continuing the wall's deep eggplant paint onto the ceiling, the couple created the illusion of an oval space. And just when your eyes have adjusted to that trippy trompe l'oeil trick, you'll swear someone is watching you....

SCARY ART DEALS On the walls, the gaze of a doe-eyed waif by Margaret Keane and the eerie ennui of the X-girl in the clothing-ad poster ($30 each at a flea market) recall those wandering eyes in haunted-house portraiture. Don't lose your head just yet: On the side table, a disembodied diver's helmet ice bucket ($25) is one of many '60s novelties that serve as sculpture. Guarding it all? A pair of fencing-foil ashtrays ($30 each at a vintage store) and an aromatic armory of '70s perfume guns—that's the Deringer model, above right—scored on eBay for $1 to $8 each.

TERRIFYING TAILORING The only alteration the spider-web chairs ($20 for six at a yard sale) needed was spider decals. A coat of Schreuder Hascolac Cinnabar enamel turned a battered brown knockoff of an antique Chinese table into a knockout. The lamp on the side table didn't work when the couple bought it, and they liked it that way. A hooked utility light from the hardware store—Pruitt says they can turn almost anything into a lamp—preserved the piece's spirit and let there be light, too.

KILLER BARGAINS The Tibetan skeleton rug cost $75 at a flea market, and the two faux leather sofas were scored from a furniture dealer in exchange for a single ill-suited contemporary one. "We found the pair in the back of a shop that otherwise only sold modern furniture," recalls Pruitt, who suggests casing out back rooms—where sellers often store pieces that aren't moving—for great deals.

It's all in the mix: Genifer Goodman and Benjamin Sohr's living room is strong enough for a man yet pretty enough for a woman—thanks to a bold, clean black-and-white background, enlivened by punchy pink details. In front of the fireplace, a pair of Bertoia diamond chairs get graphic beneath the soft pastel flowers of a flea market painting. Fanciful toile fabric has fun with the severe lines of a minimalist sofa, while floral throw pillows bring a feminine touch to the dark leather love seat.

The Mix Masters

WHAT HAPPENS when a manly man with a taste for modern moves in with a frilly femme who has a fetish for flea market finds? Two heads may be better than one, but deciding what furniture stays and what gets pitched often leads to a lot of head butting. Not for Benjamin Sohr, a graphic designer, and Genifer Goodman, a merchandising exec, whose playfully modern living room is a case study in making the marriage of two distinctly different styles work.

Yours, Mine... Ours

"We both came to the relationship with a core group of furniture," says Goodman, now the creative director for the Body Shop U.S. Sohr's pieces were modern, while Goodman's bore a passed-around patina, hard-won by years spent prowling flea markets. Neither was willing to chuck it all for the other, so they compromised and achieved a unique mix that's "far better than anything either of us would have done alone," Goodman acknowledges. Could she possibly mean the fussy black-and-white toile that suddenly looks fresh when wrapped around the clean lines of his modern sofa? Or the floral pillow that lightens the deliciously dark and worn leather love seat? A naive painting of pink flowers softens the nearby music cabinet's bold blocks of color, too. And the bare Bertoia diamond chairs strike curvaceous poses in front of the handsome—and nonworking—fireplace. The girlish touches work because the couple used a handsome black-and-white palette to give the room a graphic edge, the perfect foil for Goodman's pink obsession. As a result, their space doesn't say "his" or "hers" but rather "theirs."

A no-frills monogram gives a piped pink pillow modern flair.

PROJECT: "MAKE" YOUR OWN MONOGRAM

Goodman designed the snappy pillow on her living room sofa, monogramming it with her initial in a chic lowercase sans serif—no decorative lines, curlicues, or tails—typeface called arial. (Also check out copperplate, Parisian, Wade Sans, and Bernhard.) Although she used a professional monogrammer for this pillow, the cost bothered the "I'm all about bargain" Goodman, and she has since discovered a more economical method. She found it at the fabric store, where iron-on appliqué letters come in a surprising variety of styles and will set you back only $1.25 to $5 apiece. They're a cinch to apply—just lay the letter(s) on the fabric, cover with a thin cloth, and press with a hot iron.

A pair of gouache panels gives precious Victoriana a bit of pop art panache in Sasha Emerson's living room.

THERE'S NOTHING CHINTZY ABOUT A LIVING ROOM MADE FROM SCRAPS.

The Eccentric

A RAMBLING VICTORIAN may seem out of character for an L.A.–based decorator with a midcentury bent. However, designer Sasha Emerson is anything but predictable. Just look at the living room in her turn-of-the-century Massachusetts summer home. Emerson found the late-1800s sofa, left, at a flea market for $200, then added humor with sky blue paint and lipstick red upholstery. She made the throw pillows using vintage fabric scraps and hung an embroidered $5 flea market panel between a pair of pricey gouache paintings. As a bonus, her affordable more-is-more decor allows for worry-free experiments. "If you're not spending big bucks, there's less stress," Emerson says. "There's no guilt if something doesn't work."

Cheap Advice

No two Sasha Emerson interiors look alike—which is what keeps her clients coming back. Below, her tips for achieving one-of-a-kind style on a real person's budget:

- Look for furniture at flea markets, estate sales, restaurant-supply stores, and institutional auctions (schools, libraries, etc.). All yield unique pieces at cut-rate prices.
- Use your imagination when assigning an item a purpose. An office credenza can house a TV in the living room.
- Buy in multiples. The more you buy, the more likely vendors are to negotiate. At home, this makes it easier to use whatever you've found. One ceramic Chihuahua is a curiosity; five make a collection.
- Almost anything becomes art once it's properly framed, from a child's drawing to a silk scarf. Make a store-bought mat more interesting by covering it in fabric or wrapping paper. Save money on framing by having molding cut to size at the hardware store.
- Forget buying a pricey rug. Design your own from carpet remnants, back and bind a favorite blanket, or if the design you love is only available in doormat sizes, have enough of them stitched together to cover your floor.
- Almost any color can be mixed into a durable super-high-gloss lacquer to give cartoonish cachet to old pieces. If you can't find a premixed can of the shade you want (Emerson uses Benjamin Moore's industrial line), bring a color swatch to a paint store and ask the staff to make it for you.

Warhol meets Sister Parish: A vintage Ferris wheel (a steal at $50) and a framed scrap of fabric sit side by side.

A lair with flair: Chip Cordélli combines a rotating sampling of his collections with an unlikely blend of '50s, '60s, and '70s furniture.

WANT TO GET GOOD AT THE HUNT? SKIP STARBUCKS AND SPEND YOUR MONEY—AND TIME—AT THE FLEA MARKET.

The Collector

TO LOOK around Chip Cordelli's apple green living room is to witness a collector's mastery of decorating alchemy. "It's about finding objects that are attractive and alluring," says Cordelli, whose definition includes "anything I've never seen before." No design snob, he's willing to open his wallet if a piece opens his mind. "I still find beauty in objects that might be imitations; I learn as much as I can about them, then cast off any bad copies I once thought were cool." The stylist calls Lady Luck his decorator, with most of the furniture in his Brooklyn, New York, living room scored on the cheap—or off the street for free.

House Blend

With such a dizzying design philosophy, how does Cordelli pull it all together? He's fearless—about fusing different styles, constantly switching it up, and not taking anything too seriously. "I'm always on the hunt for things that will pack a design punch and offer better function than the stuff already in the mix," Cordelli says.

These days a '70s Italian sofa squares off with a '50s American chest of drawers, a low-slung vintage Greta Grossman boomerang chair, and a leather ottoman carted off a beachside boardwalk. Put it all on a '70s wool shag inherited from a friend and what have you got? Good lines, neutral colors, and room to sprawl out on the floor. Toss in a mod ceramic drip lamp with an uptown string shade, an enameled abstract painting ($10 at a garage sale), pool balls as objets d'art, a slew of patterned needlepoint pillows—Cordelli buys 'em whenever he sees 'em—and you've got a pad without peer. In a final masterful stroke, he gave the window moldings (caked with 100 years of paint) a swank metallic sheen with radiator paint. All the better to frame the vintage linen draperies he snagged at an estate sale.

After 13 years in the same tiny place, the intrepid collector knows how the room needs to function. Only 25 percent of his stuff is in the apartment at one time—the rest sits in a storage unit that Cordelli visits annually. Floor-to-ceiling industrial shelving, a budget version of built-ins, has replaced a low, vertical-space-wasting credenza. A smart collage of books, paintings, and quirky collections sits on the shelves and hangs from the crossbars. "Looking at open shelves should be an unexpected trail of visual treats," Cordelli says. He insists on an unfussy display so that anyone who wants to can touch the Corgi cars, Danish and Swedish glass, and Concorde memorabilia on his lighted Lucite shelves, above, which were dumped on his stoop by a friend leaving town.

IT'S OKAY TO ADOPT A STYLE À LA CARTE.

Partial Purists

FOR Nick Grad and Carolyn Bernstein, scoring their 1950s ranch house was a bonanza, until they realized that they weren't keen on midcentury furniture or its inflated price tags. But after studying up on the era's aesthetic, the couple realized that the point of postwar design was ease and accessibility—and that superstars like Eames and Noguchi weren't their only options. So they filled their living room with pieces by lesser-known names, all of which came at much lower prices.

Ranch Dressing

Nick Grad and Carolyn Bernstein's most valuable research resource wasn't some highfalutin architectural tome, but rather a 1950s *Better Homes and Gardens* guide that showed how real living rooms were put together during the period. To furnish their incarnation, the couple searched for nonpedigree pieces with elegant lines. Case in point: the sculptural rope chairs, flea market finds that only look like Hans Wegner originals. Though the sofa was designed by Jens Risom, it wasn't a pristine gallery piece when Grad and Bernstein found it, for a mere $900, at a used-furniture store. In addition to saving money by having it refurbished, the couple got to choose the perfect fabric: a stain-resistant green ultrasuede that tolerates abuse from their toddler. And that mosaic coffee table? It was just a shabby $75 tile wall hanging until a local woodworker gave it legs. At $800 each, the vintage flokati rugs weren't cheap, but they work hard—creating two distinct seating areas.

Nick Grad and Carolyn Bernstein didn't limit themselves to furniture that hailed from the '40s and '50s. The sectional sofa and matching chair on the far side of their living room are part of a '70s set. All of the pieces—still covered in original Jack Lenor Larsen fabric—cost only $2,000 at an estate sale.

Forget putting up a wall. Make one room into two—or three or four—just by shuffling the furniture around.

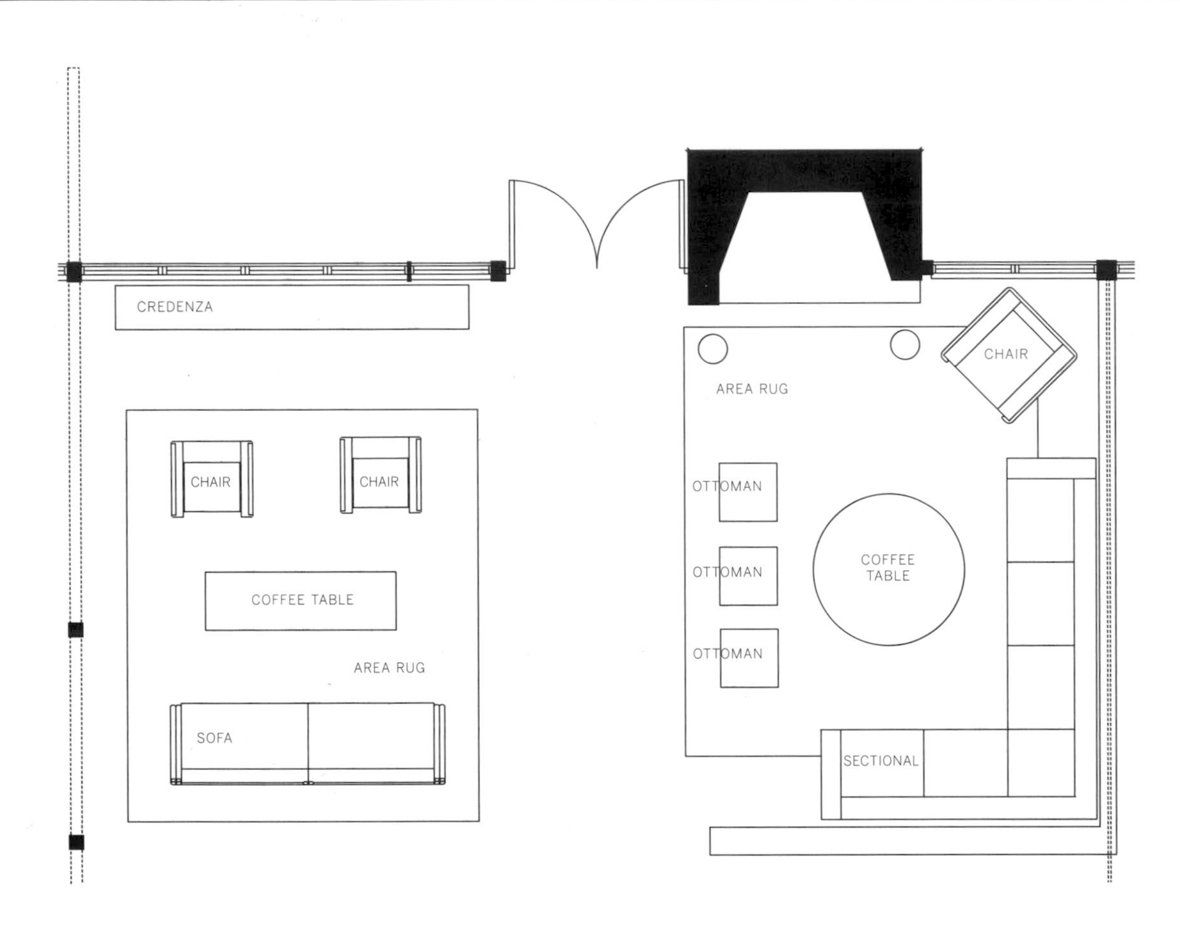

Open Discussion

Careful what you ask for: There *is* such a thing as too much space, especially when you're short on fine furniture. Try putting down two rugs, as Nick Grad and Carolyn Berstein did (above), and voilà! You have two "rooms." Small gatherings are ideal with the sofa-and-two-chairs setup on the left, while the area on the right—with its giant sectional, ottomans, and armchair—can handle a big shindig. A free-standing wall, right, separates the living room from the foyer, where a $300 garden screen provides a backdrop for a vintage needlepoint bench, $400, and a $250 flea market rug.

Making Plans

Before Grad and Bernstein began filling their living room with furniture, they called on friend and interior designer Sasha Emerson to draw up a floor plan to guide them. Good idea: Before you start on your space, take a look at Emerson's two alternate ways of laying out that same living room.

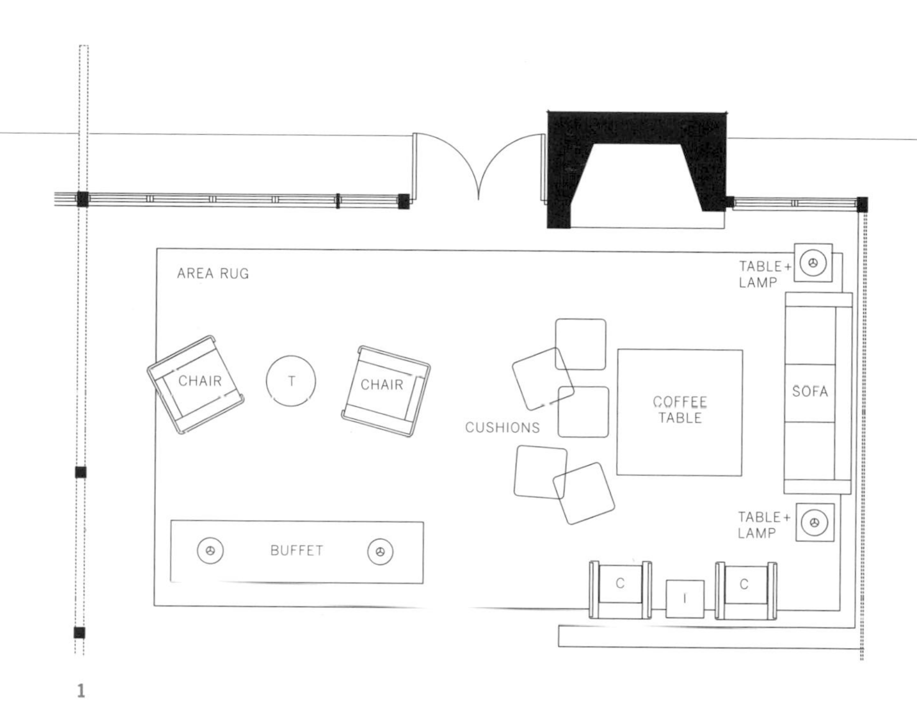

1

1. THE SPLIT PERSONALITY

Get far from the madding crowd and take in the view while you're sitting in an armchair on the left—one of four pieces of furniture that make up the "room." Or join the gang for dinner on the right; pull up a cushion, cram on the couch, or just enjoy the scene from one of the armchairs on the back wall.

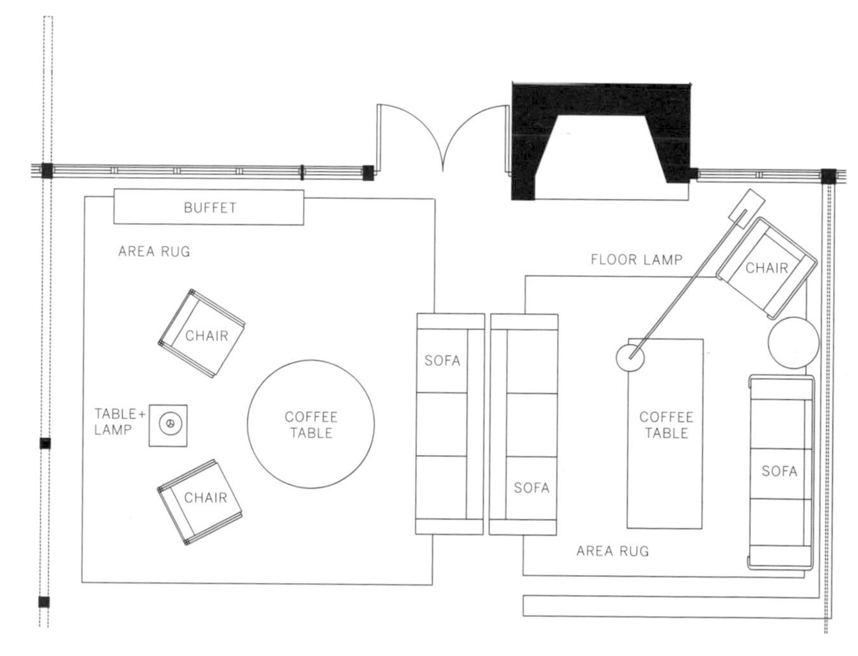

2

2. WATCH YOUR BACK

Friends not speaking to one another? They can take time out on the back-to-back couches that form a "wall" between two seating areas in a plan that accommodates a total of three sofas.

HERE'S A CHEAP WAY TO MAKE BIG DECORATING CHANGES IN A HURRY.

The Makeover

LYNNE PALAZZI and Chris Raymond were in a rut. Nothing was wrong with their marriage, but their living room had lost its spark. Unwilling to shell out for a decorator, the couple sought counseling from a different breed of design expert. Sometimes called "interior refiners," they can redo a room in a few hours using pieces you already have—for about $500. When Lauri Ward showed up, she declared the couple ahead of the curve, having made "only six or seven" common decorating mistakes (see "Ward's Top 10," page 33).

All in a Day's Work

It took Ward all of 10 minutes to point out the couple's decorating don'ts and about two hours to turn them into dos. The heaviest lift, literally, was emptying and moving the seven-foot-by-seven-foot Ikea shelving unit, below, that dominated the room. Now it's on an inside wall where it gives the dining area a library vibe. Ward also suggested reshuffling the books by stacking paperbacks horizontally in architectural towers on the bottom shelves and hardcovers on the top shelves. Next, she transformed the L-shaped living area into a more comfortable U by sliding the sofa a few feet away from the wall and placing two chairs opposite it. Ward struck a calming balance by moving the couple's most attractive pieces—an antique wooden chest of drawers and an art deco china closet—to either side of the mantel. For this refiner's final refinement, she shifted an empty gold frame that hung over the mantel, left, to the facing wall and filled it with three framed photos. In its place, Ward put a long antique mirror and surrounded it with silver candlesticks and a mirrored votive holder (see photo on page 32) to create a reflective-themed vignette. Now there's a focal point on either side of the room—and Palazzi and Raymond are free to focus on each other, instead of their decorating woes.

Interior refiner Lauri Ward freed the sofa from the wall, making the room seem larger. Behind the couch: Lynne Palazzi's collection of colored glass bottles, which had been scattered throughout the apartment. Ward also moved the huge bookcase, opposite, away from the focal point provided by the hearth and put a pretty antique chest in its place.

Ward can't say it enough: Pairs create balance. Even two small wiry topiaries on the mantel, right, do the trick. A cluster of mirrors and silver objects—all gathered from elsewhere in the apartment—shows that similar accessories have more impact when displayed together (see No. 9 on Ward's list of decorating don'ts, opposite). And there's nothing like a jumble of mismatched furniture at different heights to make a room look chopped up—especially if everything is pressed up against the walls. Just compare the "before" photo, opposite top, with the "after," opposite bottom, to see how Ward made peace with the pieces Palazzi and Raymond already owned.

Ward's Top 10

Learn Lauri Ward's 10 most common decorating mistakes, then look around your living room. Fluff it, sit back, and admire your decorating savvy.

1. Not defining your priorities: Consider whether you rent or own and how long you're going to be there. It makes a big difference when deciding where you're going to spend your money.

2. The twist and shout: If the conversation area is L-shaped, you have to twist your body and raise your voice for other people to hear you. A U shape puts you face-to-face with the person you're talking to.

3. Poor furniture placement: Pressing the furniture against the walls doesn't create more space; it just creates a big open space in the middle of the room.

4. A room that is off-balance: If you have one vertical piece in the room, add a second, like an inexpensive tree, in order to bring the eye up.

5. Furniture of different heights: Avoid the roller coaster effect. Keep your seating at one height, the artwork at another, so the room isn't visually chaotic.

6. A room that lacks a cohesive look: If there's choppiness architecturally—the doors and closets are different heights—deemphasize it by painting the walls and accents the same color. Pare down a random collection of tchotchkes by keeping just the most important pieces.

7. Ignoring the room's focal point: It could be a fireplace, a large painting, a wall unit, maybe just a picture window.

8. Improper use of artwork: Forget the "eye level" rule for hanging pictures. Hold it up where you think it should go, lower it two to three inches, and you'll have it in the right spot. Works every time.

9. Ineffective use of accessories: Keep like with like. If you have a group of photos, don't use frames of different colors, because the eye goes to the frames, not the photos. Also, bring collections together: Arrange a bunch of small things on a tray. When items are grouped, they have terrific impact.

10. Incorrect lighting: Make sure that overhead fixtures throw light down to the floor instead of up to the ceiling. Globes, for example, can create ugly shadows. Lamps should always come in pairs, and you should invest in three-way bulbs for flexibility.

Living Room Furniture

A couch, a coffee table, and a comfortable chair. If only furnishing your living room were that simple. Truth is, though, trying to find stylish pieces without spending a fortune can be exasperating. So take a look at the following pages. Get the couch you *really* want by picking up a used one and hiring an upholsterer. If you can't see the wisdom in an aged sofa, then study the new styles we've given our stamp of approval to. Does the price of a plain coffee table make you bristle? Customize it as a designer would. And when you're done, rescue a great but grimy chair. Once you see the webbed beauty in this chapter, you'll never look at a seat belt the same way again. Excited yet? Now all you need to do is turn your living room into a discreet closet. Read on.

Open-and-Shut Case

Only one tiny closet in your bedroom? Do what decorator Charles de Lisle did and turn your whole living room into a walk-in closet. Ever since de Lisle rented what just might be the smallest house in San Francisco's hip Potrero Hill neighborhood, he has been stashing his clothes in a pair of plain Ikea wardrobes that not only bring storage to his life but symmetry to his living room. The trick lies in the number *two*: One armoire would have looked like a giant elephant in the diminutive space—lopsided and purely functional. But when de Lisle set a couple of armoires on either side of an elegant midcentury bureau, he discovered just how good necessity could look—instantly the room gained a sense of depth and interest.

Want to re-cover an old couch? Do it yourself and you'll lose your mind; splurge on a pro and you'll save your sanity.

How to Spend $1,000 on a Salvation Army Sofa

It's true: You can buy a sofa at the lowliest of thrift shops and turn it into a first-class couch simply by giving it a new coat and shoes. That's what interior designer Demi Adeniran did. Anyone can find great secondhand furniture: Just look for strong well-made pieces with classic shapes—and be willing to spend more on upholstery than on the pieces themselves. She paid $150 for this sofa and a matching chair, then dropped another $1,000 to have them fitted with Lucite legs, far right, and re-covered them in a luxurious beige mohair. Yet she got a custom look for about $1,200 total, much less than a brand-new furniture set would have cost. To make such an investment last, Adeniran recommends choosing neutral fabrics for big pieces, "then play with color accents, such as pillows and throws. That way you can redecorate without going through the big expense of upholstering again."

PINNING DOWN AN UPHOLSTERER

Ever tried re-covering anything more complicated than the seat of a dining chair? According to professional upholsterer Matthew Haly, attempting complex projects by yourself is harder than it looks. Most homemade upholstery jobs rip or come undone within three months. So what will hiring a pro set you back? About $1,000 to $1,500 for a six- to seven-foot sofa, depending on where you live, the fabric you choose (plan on buying about 18 yards at a cost of at least $20 a yard), and how the sofa is built. Sure, it can be cheaper to buy a new couch, but getting a solidly built piece with the covering you really want can make the extra investment worthwhile—especially if you choose the right upholsterer. Word of mouth is a safe bet, but shop around and check references, too. Stop by a few recommended upholsterers and look at completed projects and works-in-progress. If you like what you see, return with a photo and measurements of your couch, as well as a swatch of the fabric you have in mind. Get a quote and a yardage estimate—and buy extra for repairs down the road.

1. SLIPCOVERED

2. LEATHER

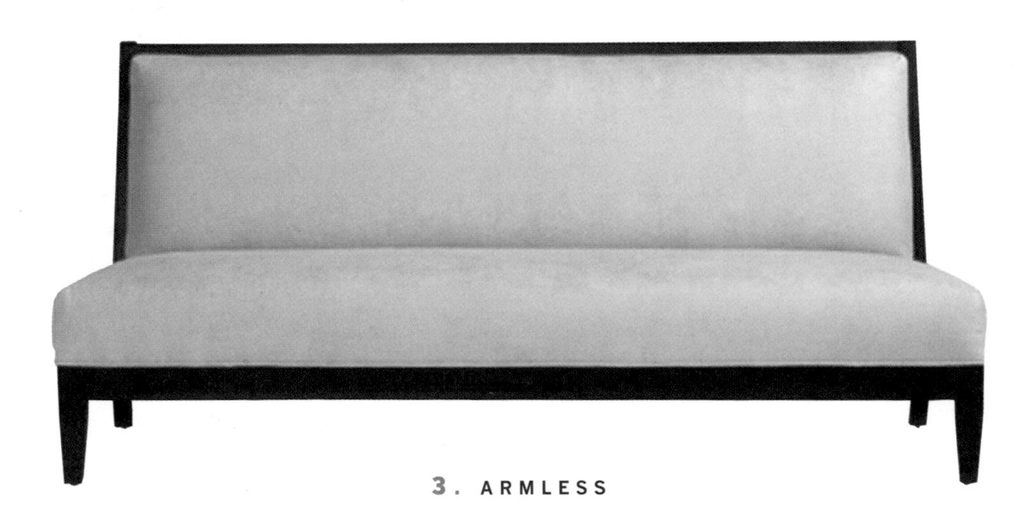

3. ARMLESS

The Goods on Sofas

If the thought of finding the perfect couch makes you want to lie down and die, give it a rest. A number of manufacturers are now making great-looking sofas in nearly every style imaginable—all at prices you can handle standing up.

1. SLIPCOVERED

If you think slipcovers mean latent stains and slouchy silhouettes, think again. With its snug-fitting cover—no sagging dust ruffle!—and modern streamlined shape, Ikea's twin-cushioned Nikkala is a white sofa even spill-prone types can live with.

2. LEATHER

Masculine, yes, but she'll like it, too. Handsome lines, a dark brown hue, and tasteful French upholstery nails separate this Roots two-seater from the pack of bad black bachelor-pad clichés. Plus, its chocolate leather has the kind of classic good looks that age well.

3. ARMLESS

This bench seat is so chic, it doesn't need such superfluous details as arms. The appeal of this Room & Board baby lies in its bare nakedness—no fabric bunching up

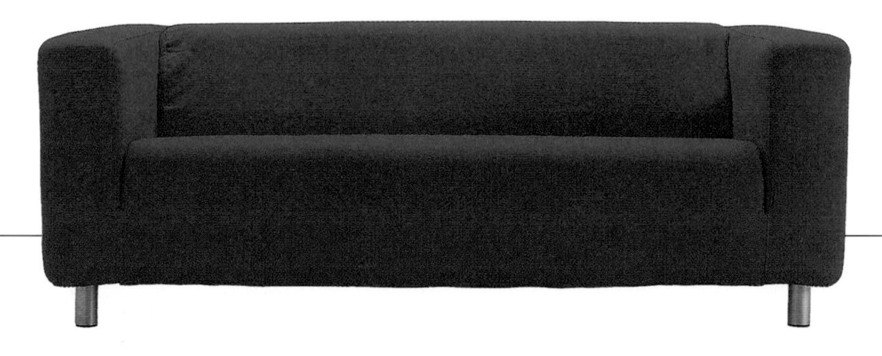

4. PETITE

5. DAYBED

6. CONVERTIBLE

at the corners, no valance shifting around the legs. Even better, this design plays it both ways, fitting in easily with either traditional or modern decorating schemes.

4. PETITE

Want something roomier than a love seat but smaller than a sofa? Ikea's six-foot Klippan is easily the cheapest solution on the market. And should you tire of that bold red fabric, the company sells sensibly priced slipcovers in six other shades.

5. DAYBED

The tufts make it tough to do anything but get horizontal on West Elm's low sofa. The East-meets-West design—that steel base fits a standard twin mattress—provides Zen calm without sacrificing comfort. It's the best thing to happen to the siesta since, well, the mid-morning nap.

6. CONVERTIBLE

Bring back fond memories of your college futon—without the accompanying back pain and dubious dormitory decor. The magic of this multitasker by Bo Concept is that it looks as good when you're lying down as it does when you're standing up. Pull out this Danish design for your friends and they may never leave.

The Inside Scoop

When architect Stephen Atkinson designed a weekend cottage outside Baton Rouge, Louisiana, for his mother and father, the family blew most of its tiny budget on the building itself and ended up with hardly any money for the interior. So Brenda and John Atkinson headed to Pier One Imports, where they found two rattan porch chairs—at less than $150 apiece—that look smart enough to sit inside their getaway. Cozied up with patterned throw pillows from West Elm, the generously proportioned pair are as welcoming as any stuffed armchairs. With a little help from a set of Ikea nesting tables and a sisal carpet layered with a nubby area rug, the made-for-the-outdoors duo is decidedly at home inside. For other interior-worthy exterior furniture, check out your local garden center, flea markets, and mass-market retailers like Kmart and Target. A wicker settee can make a great living room love seat, and why not put a poolside chaise in your living room and call it a modern-day fainting couch?

Orange Crush

Got a chair that looks a little too bottomed out to sit in your living room? This webbed workhorse had been passed down so much, it's a wonder the arms only had a few scratches and the webbed seat was only slightly stained. After determining that it was not an original Alvar Aalto No. 45 (worth big bucks), we set to work on a bold face-lift. We removed the webbing, using pliers to pry out its fasteners, and disassembled the frame for easier painting. After sanding the wood, brushing on a few coats of white high-gloss latex, and letting it dry overnight, we reassembled the frame. Guided by the original webbing, we cut bright orange seat belt straps (scored on eBay for $10) to the proper lengths, then painted clear nail polish over the ends to prevent fraying. We attached the horizontal straps to both sides of the frame with a heavy-duty staple gun. Then we stapled the vertical straps to the top of the frame and wove them in and out of the horizontal bands, pulling the straps taut and stapling them at the bottom. Now the chair has a nice tight seat, and we're sitting pretty.

What would a designer do? Four of the hottest names in the business sex up a timid living room staple.

1. THE TALKER

2. THE FASHIONISTA

THE ORIGINAL

Turning the Tables

It's not that this clean modern decor staple really needs anything. But despite its tasteful simplicity—or perhaps because of it—the politely plain and jaw-droppingly cheap Ikea birch-veneer Lack coffee table sometimes seems a little, well, lacking. We sent the staid table packing to a group of today's hottest designers—of furniture, interiors, gardens, and such—then asked them to transform this decor essential by way of ingenuity and resourcefulness, not the ATM.

1. Talk about a conversation piece. Mark Naden, an architect and industrial designer, decided to riff on the awkwardly polite chitchat that often occurs around a coffee table. So, jigsaw in hand, he sliced the top of the Lack into 18 equal-size chunks. On the sides of each segment, he glued white plastic laminate, silk-screened with multiple sayings such as YOU LOOK GREAT!, IS THAT POSSIBLE?, and IT WAS BRILLIANT!, and then attached individual drawer runners to the bottoms. The effect? Total interactivity, with movable phrases that slide back and forth, mimicking dialogue between two

3. THE ARTIST

4. THE EXTROVERT

people. And just like cocktail party conversation, the piece is infinitely reconfigurable.

2. Interior architect Henry Mitchell's interpretation is one of snazzy refinement, created with patterned fabric, which Mitchell attached with a staple gun. He also sawed off the Lack's legs, then screwed on Ikea's Capita chrome numbers because "if the table's lower, the style is more timeless." The result: cheap, easy glam that's so stunning, Mitchell is making more for himself.

3. Jean Klebs, a mixed-media artist, was in her studio when she glanced over at her art supplies and found inspiration. Klebs brought some oomph to humble hardware-store paintbrushes by sawing them in half and applying cherry red paint. For the table itself, she achieved a rustic yet graphic feel with a solid blue stripe and a piney wood grain, courtesy of a faux-finish kit.

4. Floral, garden, and interior designer Rebecca Cole enlivened the Lack with a splash of bold orange color. For her funky creation, the always-fearless cohost of the Discovery Channel's *Surprise by Design* opted for Day Glo vinyl, tempered with practicality: a handy pocket with a button closure holds the remote. Plus, the lima bean–shaped plywood overlay is removable, "so you can revert to the original Ikea top when the in-laws visit," she explains. Not that Cole will be doing a switcheroo anytime soon. She has proudly installed the piece, mod side on, in her SoHo brownstone's living room—even though it required reupholstering the couch.

Living Room Lighting

Finding the right lamp is a tall order when you consider the number of options that are beamed at you like a thousand points of light. To get it right, you often need to see how a piece works in *your* living room. But who can afford to load up on lamps just to see which one does the job best? You can. With the variety of cheap designer knockoffs available, even self-respecting stingy souls can make mistakes without feeling fiscally unfit. One look at the choices in this section and you'll see just how easy it is to light up your life without losing your shirt. If you can't bear the thought of buyer's remorse, make your own. It's as easy as the flip of a bucket. Or use cheap plastic plates to create a pop art sconce that would make any penny-pincher proud.

Adapting to the Light

Indeed, it's the small things that can change your life. And for a little more than small change you can turn almost anything into a cool lamp shade.

To make the machine-age beauty at left, all you need is a cheap metal ice bucket, a clip-on adapter, and a cap nut (about $1 for eight) from the hardware store. 1. Drill a quarter-inch hole in the center of the bottom of the ice bucket. 2. Slide the clip-on adapter over your lamp's bulb and place the inverted bucket over the adapter. 3. Screw a 10-24-size acorn cap nut onto the adapter to serve as a finial.

To make the spirographic sconce, above, we used two daisy-shaped plastic plates and that same clip-on adapter and cap nut. 1. Drill a quarter-inch hole in the center of each plate. 2. Insert the clip-on adapter through both holes from the back of the plates. Follow step 3, above, and flip the switch.

Can't see shelling out for a designer lamp? Look on the bright side: There's a look-alike that's easy on your eyes *and* your wallet.

1. CLASSIC

2. MINIMALIST

3. ZEN

Make Light of It

If the cold antiseptic glare of a harsh overhead gives you the chills, there's a better way to bring a little cheap and flattering light into your life. Just scatter a few table lamps around the room and bask in their soothing ambient glow. With so many styles available, it's easy to be blinded by their sheer numbers. How do you choose? Light on a designer style you love, study its lines and details, and look for the closest fake you can find.

1. CLASSIC

Want that uptown decorator look without making a down payment on it? Leave it to Martha Stewart to create a glossy globe that oozes European boutique elegance without the inflated continental cost. Hers hails from Kmart, but Wal-Mart, Target, and other mass-market retailers carry similar ceramic versions at equally palatable prices.

2. MINIMALIST

Can't decide between steely minimalism and warm rustic charm? You don't have to choose. A simple streamlined base like this one (from Associated West Imports) can handle practically any pattern you pick for its shade. From faux bois to floral, polka dots to plaid, you can change the mood in your living room with a simple switch. Crate and Barrel, Pottery Barn, and PBteen usually offer versions of this style shifter.

3. ZEN

Hey, paper pushing isn't only for eggheads. If a lamp is as enlightening as this egg-

4. INDUSTRIAL

5. KITSCHY

6. FEMININE

shaped Noguchi knockoff, then it can't be a bad way to get turned on. This Asian charmer will give your living room a gorgeous glow without burning a hole in your wallet. Check out the look-alikes at Urban Outfitters, Ikea, and PearlRiver.com.

4. INDUSTRIAL

The ubiquitous metal desk lamp may not be all that original—in an office. But pull this hardworking fixture out of its natural habitat and you'll see it in a whole new light—chic, practical, industrial. Place a pair on either end of a sofa: Propped up by a short stack of books, they'll make stylish reading lamps. Although this Martha Stewart version came from Kmart, you can also find 'em at almost any decor or office-supply store.

5. KITSCHY

Bored with your decor? Forget your troubles and go on, get happy, with a lamp that will bring a little humor into your living room. What Yayo Designs' quirky doe-eyed deer lacks in taste it makes up for in cheap thrills. Not fond of Bambi? Troll eBay and flea markets for other members of the animal kingdom.

6. FEMININE

Who said girls shouldn't be bold? If timid floral fabrics leave you longing for something louder, check out the three-dimensional silk roses on Maura Daniel's white swirl drum shade. It ain't too shabby-looking set atop a chic crystal base. This combination is admittedly costly, but it blows the petals off those blowsy garden roses synonymous with the overblown '80s.

Living Room Walls & Floors

If your living room walls could talk, would they yawn? Have you left them bare in hopes of scoring that signed Seurat at the flea market? Go ahead and dream, but in the meantime, there's no reason to be bored by the surfaces that surround you. One look at the ideas on the following pages, and you'll wake up to the truth. Some of the most clever coverings cost less than a can of paint. Others ask little more of you than recalling your paper-folding skills from kindergarten. After you handle your ho-hum walls, hit the floor. Forget the pricey Aubusson carpet and go for remnants, which you can have cut and edged on the cheap. Or try carving a zebra skin rug out of vinyl floor covering. Whichever you chose, the feeling underfoot—and in your wallet—will be pure bliss.

Yes, But Is It Art?

Got really big blank walls and a teeny tiny budget? There's no point in pining away for that Rauschenberg, but that doesn't mean the space above your sofa needs to stay empty forever, either. Although neon-lit beer ads are a dorm-room decorating cliché, there is sophisticated signage out there. The four relief Rotary and Kiwanis signs at left—picked up at a flea market for a total of $250—provide a more grown-up graphic boost.

Sticklers for real art won't know the difference when you hang a takeoff of Grant Wood's iconic American couple, above, in an ornate frame stuck to the wall. Getting the decal made is far cheaper than taking your art to a professional framer: For around $50, most sign shops will make a poster-size sticker. Bring a design of the correct size, either on paper or CD, and they'll run it through a decalmaker. The best source for frame designs is Dover Publications' clip-art CDs, in particular *372 Frames and Borders* and *Old-Fashioned Frames* (approximately $10 each at Amazon.com).

Welcome to the Fold

Forget origami. You don't need to fold 1,000 cranes for good luck when a quick turn of the page will transform your secret stash of guilty-pleasure hardcovers into cutting-edge art. Inspired by artist Mary Bennett, whose work is exhibited at Santa Fe's Evo Gallery, we had copies of our favorite reads folded and hung in no time. To create the top look, fold the upper corner of a page down and tuck it into the center crease of the book, then fold the bottom corner of the next page into the crease of the book. Once you've folded all the pages, display the book using a seven-inch plate hanger. For directions on creating the middle and bottom looks, check out the step-by-step photos on the following page.

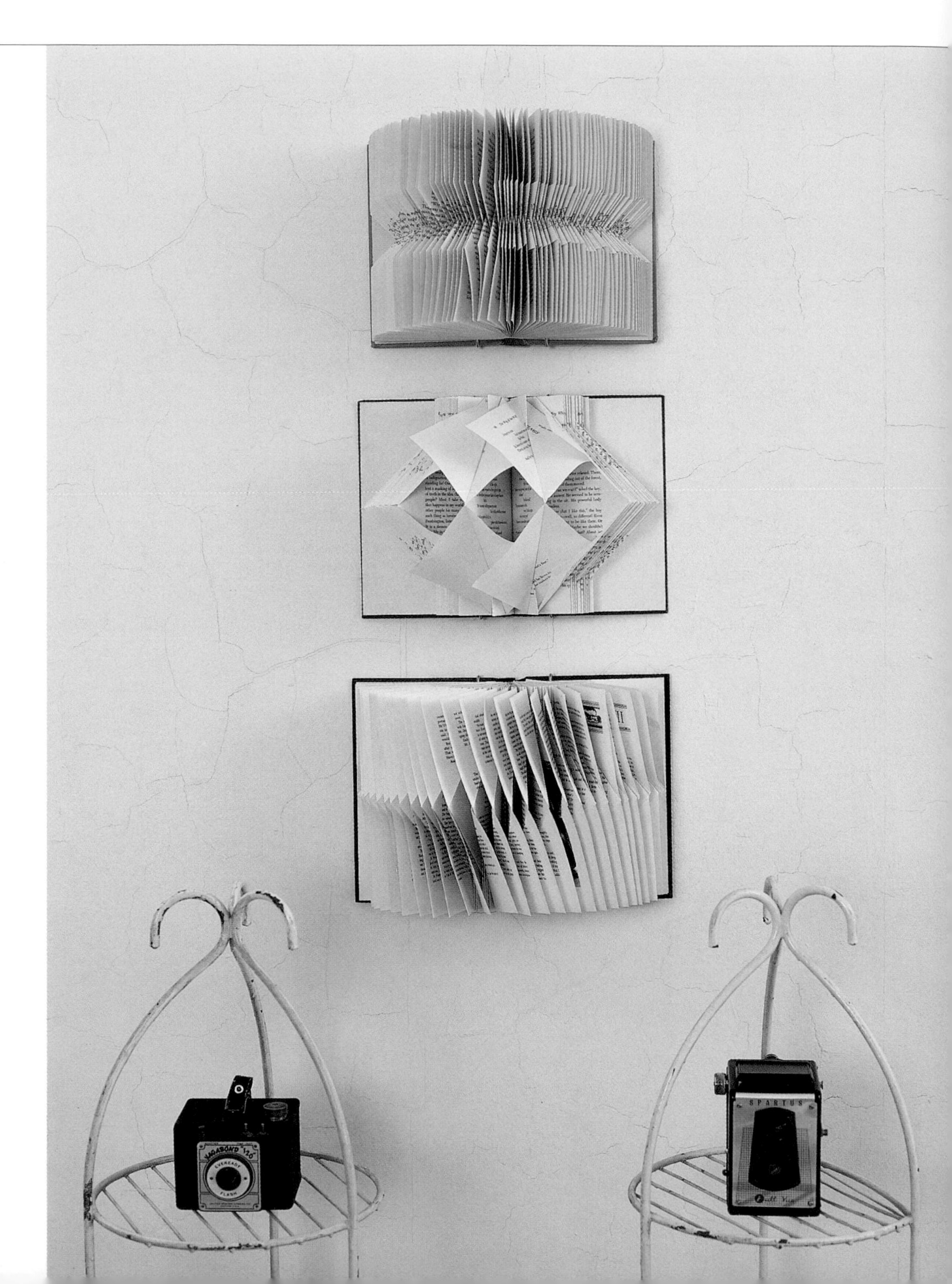

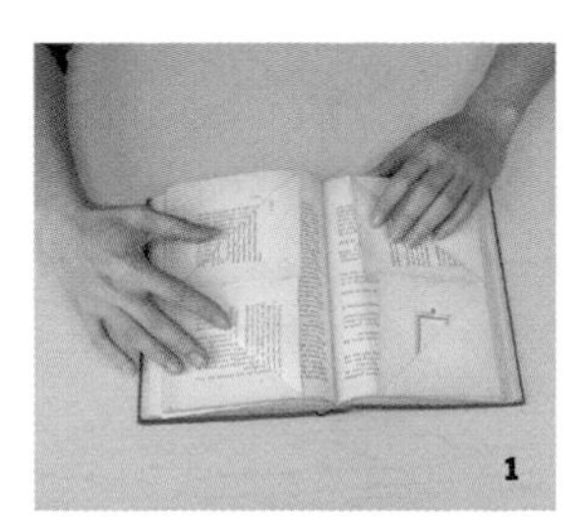

PROJECT:

DIAMONDS ARE FOREVER

(middle book)

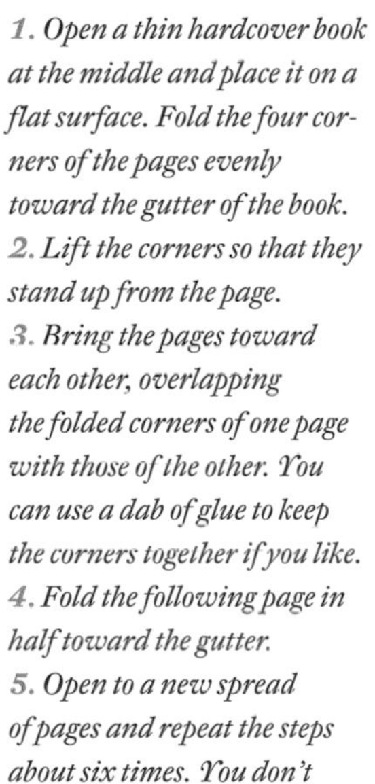

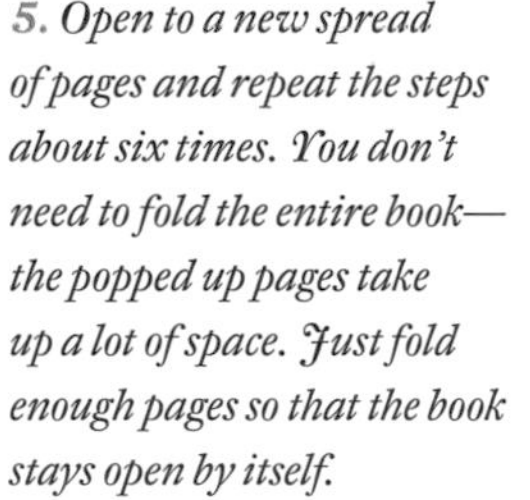

1. Open a thin hardcover book at the middle and place it on a flat surface. Fold the four corners of the pages evenly toward the gutter of the book.
2. Lift the corners so that they stand up from the page.
3. Bring the pages toward each other, overlapping the folded corners of one page with those of the other. You can use a dab of glue to keep the corners together if you like.
4. Fold the following page in half toward the gutter.
5. Open to a new spread of pages and repeat the steps about six times. You don't need to fold the entire book—the popped up pages take up a lot of space. Just fold enough pages so that the book stays open by itself.

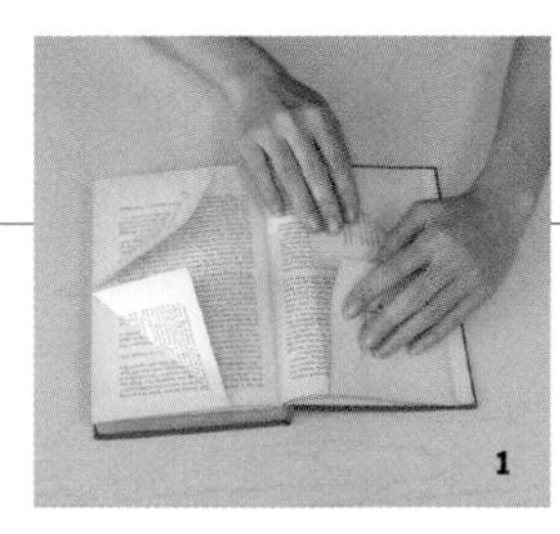

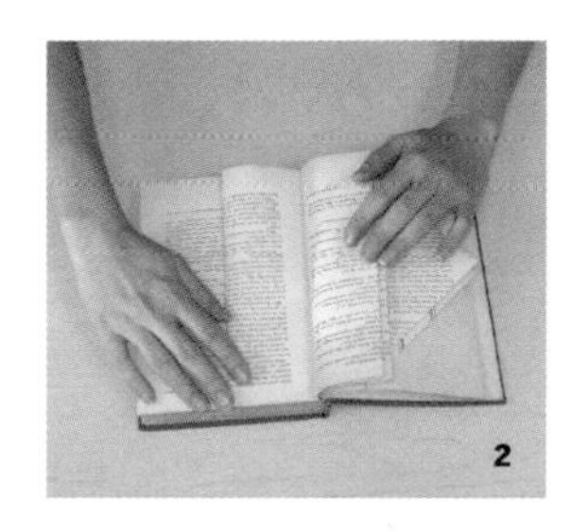

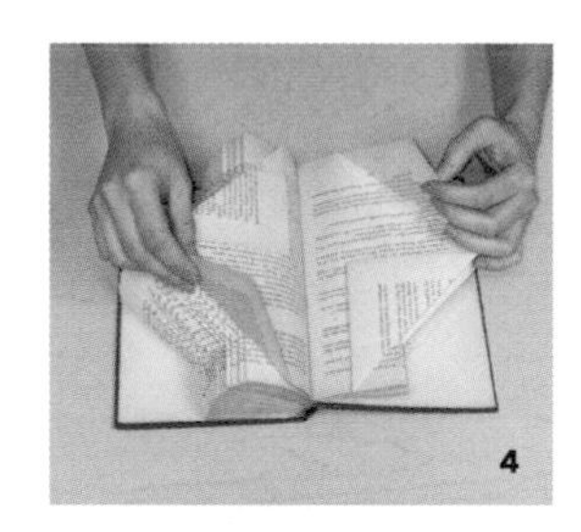

PROJECT:

LITERARY TWIST

(bottom book)

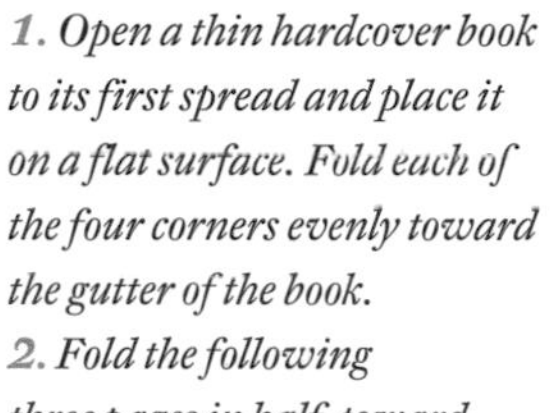

1. Open a thin hardcover book to its first spread and place it on a flat surface. Fold each of the four corners evenly toward the gutter of the book.
2. Fold the following three pages in half, toward the gutter.
3. Open to the next spread of pages. Repeat steps 1 and 2 until you've folded all of the pages in the book.
4. Once you've finished folding, open the book to the spread closest to the front cover that has folded corners. Lift two corners that diagonally face each other so that they stand up from the page.
5. Bring the two pages together. The lifted corners should stick out from the sides. Repeat steps 4 and 5 for the rest of the pages with folded corners.

PROJECT:
DARK SHADOWS

"The mixture of the real and the unreal is nicely unsettling," says painter Rob Pruitt of the fake shadows he and his partner, conceptual artist Jonathan Horowitz, cast on the walls of their sprawling 1895 Victorian. The black silhouette of the bird lamp in the living room, above, is scarily simple to re-create in your home: Shine a very bright light onto a lamp or any other object, then trace the outer edge of the shaded area on the wall and fill it with flat finish latex paint. Much like the bird shadow, the wrought iron fence effect, left, was created by projecting the design of a cresting (a Victorian widow's walk ornament) downloaded from the Web. Pruitt and Horowitz shone the image on the wall using an old-school overhead projector (borrow one from your local library or a teacher friend), then traced its outline and painted within the line. The Gothic fence is the perfect backdrop for showcasing the couple's dark sense of humor: Darth Vader hangs on the wall, overlooking his likeness in a shampoo bottle next to a cheap whiskey bust—"I'm your Old Grand-Dad, Luke."

Deep Frieze

When did wallpaper get so damn wild? The bucolic scene, left, is actually a photo mural that costs far less than a getaway vacation to such a pristine locale. Environmental Graphics has got you covered with its bank of thousands of images. Wish you could get out of the city and breathe some fresh air? Check out Morning Forest. Want to bone up on your geography with one eye on the tube? Plaster your living room walls with the Executive World Map. You can go to the desert, the seashore, the moon, or back to the farm just by clicking your way to EG's website (www.muralsmyway.com). The company also offers a service that will turn anything—your photo, your child's artwork—into larger-than-life wall coverings. Whatever you chose, hang it with a clear strippable ready-mix adhesive such as Golden Harvest GH-34.

Cover your floor with cut-rate carpet? Of course. Clip a sharp skin out of a linoleum look-alike? Sure.

Clever Covers

The remnant bin is ripe with cheap floor covering possibilities like the "pool of blood" carpet, left, spilling down the stairs in Rob Pruitt and Jonathan Horowitz's Gothic mansion. The 100-foot-long runner cost them $1,400, including having it custom-cut and edged on site. Opposite: For a cheaper alternative, transform a vinyl remnant—a six-square-foot piece will run you around $25—into a sharp zebra skin in less than a day. How? Ask a friend to lay spread-eagle on the vinyl and trace your pal's outline, tweaking it until it resembles the shape at right. Then cut it out with heavy-duty scissors. Paint the back side of the vinyl with two coats of latex-based white primer. When dry, draw the stripes on freehand (use our example as a guide or Google *zebra skin rug* for a reference image). Fill in the bands with two coats of gloss black latex (we used Rust-Oleum's Painter's Touch), let 'em dry, and give the whole thing a protective coat of polyacrylic. Wait a couple days, then walk proudly on your new rug.

GUCCI
GUCCI

2

Don't be tempted to cook the books to score that designer kitchen you crave. Stick to your budget and avoid getting stuck with a cookie-cutter look by customizing your cupboards, painting your appliances, or turning a kitchen island into a dining room table.

Kitchens & Dining

A kitchen redo can be so costly that many of us skip it entirely, turning a blind eye to outdated appliances, crummy cabinets, and dingy linoleum floors. But there is some middle ground between doing nothing and blowing a fortune—and the designers and home owners in this chapter have found it. Instead of buying all new appliances, why not paint that avocado green fridge? (It's easier than you think.) Same goes for those clunky cupboards: A coat of high-gloss enamel can work wonders when it comes to hiding cheesy faux wood grains, though sometimes all that's needed is a fresh set of hardware. And why erect a wall when a simple curtain is enough to keep those dirty dishes out of sight? Once you've feasted your eyes on this section's clever kitchen fixes, take a seat in the dining room. We've got six super chair styles, all less than $200 apiece, as well as some ideas for ways to refresh older models. For that all-important table: Whatever you do, don't buy a perfectly restored period piece—not when you can nab a run-down antique, pay to have it refinished, and still come out ahead. Sick of searching for a crystal chandelier you can actually afford? Then check out the elegant D.I.Y. fixture on page 62 or peruse the roundup of unexpected pendant lamp ideas on page 85. These shining examples will have you seeing your wastebasket, colander, and paint cans in a whole new light. What are you waiting for? Go ahead, eat it up.

KIN
moviefone
digitalcity

The Vintage Pull

I'm always amazed when I go into people's houses and they've just bought the latest thing," says interior designer Sasha Emerson, right. "I'd much rather have something unique." She's sincere, right down to the tiniest detail, like her vintage drawer pulls and knobs. Although it's easy to find a few of these charmers at flea markets, landing a full set is nearly impossible. Emerson called on the folks at Liz's Antique Hardware in Los Angeles to round out her collection. They also offer the chic black-and-ivory number at top. As for the rest of the knobs and pulls above, they're part of the stash available at HistoricHouseparts.com.

A LITTLE VISION, NOT A LOT OF MONEY, IS ALL IT TAKES TO PULL OFF A FAST FACE-LIFT.

The Quick Fix

WHEN SASHA EMERSON and Larry Levin bought their Massachusetts country house, the kitchen was your typical 1970s nightmare of dark brown cabinets, fake brass hardware, and filthy beige countertops. In less than seven days—and with little more than $3,000—Emerson transformed the room from floor to ceiling. Here's a play-by-play of how she pulled it off:

The Countdown

Most mortals can't even plan a dinner party in a week, but the spirited Emerson transformed her entire kitchen in that time frame. According to the bargain-savvy decorator, setting a tough deadline for herself was actually a plus, because it forced her to make fast decisions, eliminating the usual hemming and hawing.

1 FLOOR Linoleum may conjure images of sitcom kitchens or high school hallways, but this eco-friendly material has undergone a serious overhaul: It's now available in a range of modern colors and patterns at your local floor and tile dealer. Emerson's $350 total included 80 square feet of tile plus the cost of professional installation.

2 CABINETS Not a fan of faux oak? Paint rather than replace the offending surfaces. Emerson used Benjamin Moore's Decorator White II in a semigloss oil enamel, which is more durable than latex. She found plastic drawer pulls at a flea market for $5 each, then had the matching service at Liz's Antique Hardware (www.lahardware.com) track down similar knobs for the cabinets. She spent $208 ($70 for the hardware, $30 for a gallon of primer, $68 for two gallons of paint, and $40 for painting supplies).

3 COUNTERTOPS Emerson blew most of her budget on azurine, a blue-flecked marble. Don't have the funds for such big rocks? She recommends white laminate (about $30 per linear foot) or Corian (around $70 per *installed* square foot at Home Depot). Her $2,000 tab encompassed $750 for two marble slabs and $1,250 for polishing and installation.

4 BACKSPLASH Mexican glass tiles come in many colors and sizes. Emerson opted for square green tiles at $9 a square foot and paid $350 to have them installed, for a total of $550.

5 WALLS AND CEILING Emerson juxtaposed the bold tiles and bright cabinets with a muted gray green from Benjamin Moore called Grey Mirage. One gallon cost $25.

6 SEATING Emerson found four old dinette stools, each $70, at an L.A. antiques store, then paid $100 to have them powder-coated green and another $120 to have them re-covered in blue leather for a total of $500. To get the look for less, she recommends spray-painting your old vintage stools with Rust-Oleum (about $6 per can) and using a staple gun to reupholster the seats yourself.

Organic meets industrial: Highly polished floors and a richly colored table and chairs (unearthed at a New York City thrift shop) mix seamlessly with stainless steel appliances and stark white countertops.

TEARING DOWN A WALL CAN TURN A DIM KITCHEN INTO A DESIGNER'S DELIGHT.

The Galley Gone Grand

WITH THE SWING of a sledgehammer, Demi Adeniran liberated herself from the dark galley kitchen she inherited when she bought her modest New York City apartment. By taking down a wall, the designer created an elegant, open space large enough to hold her vintage dining table and chairs. Of course, she also got a view from thc living room. So Adeniran chose appliances worth staring at—sleek but affordable stainless steel models—and kept unsightly necessities undercover in slender frost-fronted cabinets.

Mass Can Be Marvelous

A major component of Adeniran's decorating strategy is to buy inexpensive standard items and customize them. For example, take her slick kitchen cabinets. The backs are cheap Formica units from Ikea, but Adeniran gave them a face-lift by adding doors made of a new industrial plastic that looks just like frosted glass, only it costs less, doesn't break, and never shows fingerprints. Finding the material (not to mention the hardware and steel edging that hides the cabinets' Formica underpinnings) required a lot of research but was well worth the effort.

Used to be, you could either spend a fortune on professional stainless steel or put up with boring white (or, worse, bad avocado) plastic. But in the past few years a number of accessible manufacturers—including Kenmore, Frigidaire, KitchenAid, and GE—have begun offering appliances that deliver Sub-Zero charm without all those extra zeros on the price tag. Adeniran's modern dishwasher and 16-cubic-foot fridge, from Frigidaire and Summit, respectively, came in at only $400 and $750. The designer's $950 Frigidaire gas stove cost a bit more, but its fancy internal broiler keeps her in roasted sweet corn all summer long.

Get a professional look without the big price: GE's CleanSteel fridge, left, costs around $700; Frigidaire's stainless steel stove, above, under $600.

PROJECT: STEAL THIS BRIGHT IDEA

Once Adeniran accepted the fact that she couldn't afford the $750 light fixture she'd been ogling at Moss (Murray Moss's cutting-edge Manhattan boutique), she decided to make her own chandelier. How did she do it? **1.** *The designer started with half-silver bulbs ($4.50 to $8, depending on size), below left, and sketched out a design that incorporates bulbs of various sizes.* **2.** *She scoured hardware stores until she found white ceramic fittings for $2.25 each, then hit a high-end lighting shop for white silk electrical cord ($1.50 per yard).* **3.** *Since Adeniran draws the D.I.Y. line at electrical wiring, she took the design and components to an electrician, who assembled the fixture and installed it above her dining room table, opposite. Total cost: $75.*

The Nonconformists

THINK ALL KITCHENS have to be sterile, sparkling-white industrial workhorses? Artists Rob Pruitt and Jonathan Horowitz certainly don't. They decorated the room just like the rest of their Gothic mansion in upstate New York—with dark irony and an offbeat mix of new bargains and antique finds. The results are killer, but the cost didn't make the couple keel over. By painting the walls (and appliances!), bargain hunting, and simply daring to be different, they created a kitchen that leaves guests green with envy.

With forest green walls, a vintage stove, and butler's mirror, the kitchen is as elegant as any living room. A $40 butcher block table, right, became a style statement even Morrissey could love.

Acid Taste

Ever try to make an old fridge look cool? When Pruitt and Horowitz bought their house, "the appliances were a mishmash of colors: one white, one harvest gold, one olive green," Horowitz says. But instead of replacing the existing refrigerator with a pricey brushed-aluminum model—which wouldn't have fit with the house's look (or budget)—they opted to paint the existing fridge acid green. "I'm a painter, so I wasn't intimidated by it," Pruitt says, "but a lot of people are reluctant to paint appliances." Don't be; it's surprisingly simple. First, lightly sand the appliance's exterior with medium-grit (150) sandpaper; thoroughly rinse the surface and allow to dry. Next, give it a coat of metal primer and let dry overnight. Then, using a foam roller, apply an even coat of oil-based enamel and allow it to dry overnight. Pruitt swears by Dutch brand Schreuder's metal primer AC and Hascolac Brilliant paint, though Rust-Oleum's metal primer and any marine-quality enamel will also do the job.

Rob Pruitt and Jonathan Horowitz put that trailer park staple, the tire planter, atop their painted fridge and filled it with fake pumpkins for a year-round Halloween feel. The plastic cleavers are cut-rate finds from Wal-Mart's costume aisle.

The Retro

MOST PEOPLE would have pitched this old stove the minute they moved in, but Genifer Goodman took it as a sign that the place was meant for her. Passionate about all things vintage, she made the chrome-trimmed beauty the center of attention.

Take Me, I'm Yours

Goodman was so thrilled to find this '50s stove in her rental house that she decided to make it the focal point of the kitchen. Treating the old cooker as if it were a mantelpiece, Goodman uses it to display a quirky and ever-changing assortment of bargains. Lining the back of the stove in this picture: blocks from a Swiss museum store, hot pink straws picked up on a Mexican vacation, and flowers blooming in an inexpensive Ikea pot. Behind the stove, cardboard birds ($4 at a novelty shop) flutter above a $20 thrift shop clock. The bold floral '60s curtain was a flea market find.

If you inherit a vintage stove the way Goodman did, consider yourself lucky. A properly restored model like hers can run anywhere from $4,500 to $5,500. Still interested? Log on to VintageStoves.com or StoveHospital.com to peruse the selection. But beware of dirt-cheap stoves at online auctions. According to the folks at VintageStoves.com, it's easy to get burned. If a price seems too good to be true, it probably is. What to look out for? Make sure the stove is *fully functioning*; fully restored does not necessarily mean the piece is in mint, or even working, condition.

Task lighting: Genifer Goodman fastened an office swivel lamp (around $25) to the windowsill to provide light that the hoodless stove couldn't. Opposite: Goodman can't pass up pink flowers. Her collection of melamine dishware is an eclectic mix of floral patterns and solids; she usually pays around $2 for each piece.

PROJECT: SCALING THE WALLS

"I can stay up all night sewing," says Chantal Dussouchaud. Her inspiration: a Le Corbusier quote stenciled on a blank canvas. Beneath it is a desk Dussouchaud bought for $75 at a Salvation Army and freshened up with a coat of white paint. Its generous size allows her to comfortably make large pieces like the floor-to-ceiling drapes and wall hanging, right, which is actually an oversize Roman shade. For a similar look, you could buy a store-bought window covering, but you won't get to choose the fabrics and size you want. Besides, anyone who can work a sewing machine pedal can make a simple version of this graphic piece in one day: Bind three panels together by sewing two straight seams, then press. On either side of the piece, double-turn a half inch to the reverse; press and stitch. Make a channel at the bottom and the top: Double-turn one inch and stitch closed. Insert a half-inch wooden dowel into each channel, then mount on the wall.

The magic touch: You'd never guess from the sleek look of Chantal Dussouchaud's dining room that she made most of its accessories herself.

THE THINGS YOU MAKE YOURSELF ALWAYS HAVE MORE MEANING.

The Craftswoman

"I LOVE SEWING AND SAWING," says French-born interior decorator Chantal Dussouchaud. And nowhere is her handiwork more evident than in the dining room of the Hollywood Hills home she shares with her husband, Harry Dolman. Usually a roomful of D.I.Y. projects results in cloying country-craft cuteness, but here the effect is refined—even minimal—because everything is filtered through Dussouchaud's unerring eye.

Haute and Homemade

Dussouchaud's clients are often shocked when she proposes items from Ikea instead of, say, Herman Miller or Donghia, but for this interior expert, good design is good design. And when coupled with an affordable price tag, it usually wins out. Although the designer does splurge—in her own home that meant a Viking range and fine porcelain for her many dinner parties—she compensates for it by making or remaking things herself. "I love transforming objects and finding new purposes for them," Dussouchaud says. "When you change something, you make it your own, not just something you bought." The dining room table illustrates her point perfectly. The stainless steel–topped table was a tall kitchen island from Restoration Hardware until Dussouchaud cut it down to dinner-party size, using a handsaw to take five inches off each leg. The fringe-trimmed linen drapes are another of the designer's favorite projects. She sewed them herself, then applied the grommets using a kit (available at hardware stores for around $20) and threaded them onto a simple stainless steel rod. When it came to the walls, the budget-minded Dussouchaud practiced what she often preaches to her clients: You don't need expensive art to cover your walls. She took to her sewing machine again, this time to make a two-tone wall hanging gorgeous enough to inspire even a novice seamstress to take up needle and thread (see instructions, opposite). Then, in a nod to her homeland, the decorator hung pairs of French postcards in simple wooden frames she picked up at a garage sale, and then updated with a fresh coat of paint. When Dussouchaud does buy new things, she seeks out pieces that are, first and foremost, well crafted. "That means that I occasionally will spend on furniture that's a bit pricey," she says, referring to her Alias Highframe dining chairs by Italian designer Alberto Meda. At $560 each, they may seem out of character for the frugal Frenchwoman, but she does stand by her cheap good-design dictum: She hung a sleek aluminum pendant lamp, which cost less than $10 at Ikea, over the table.

Pattern, not color, enlivens Carolyn Bernstein and Nick Grad's dining room. One exception: the bold blue Raymor pottery that fills the couple's Danish modern wall unit.

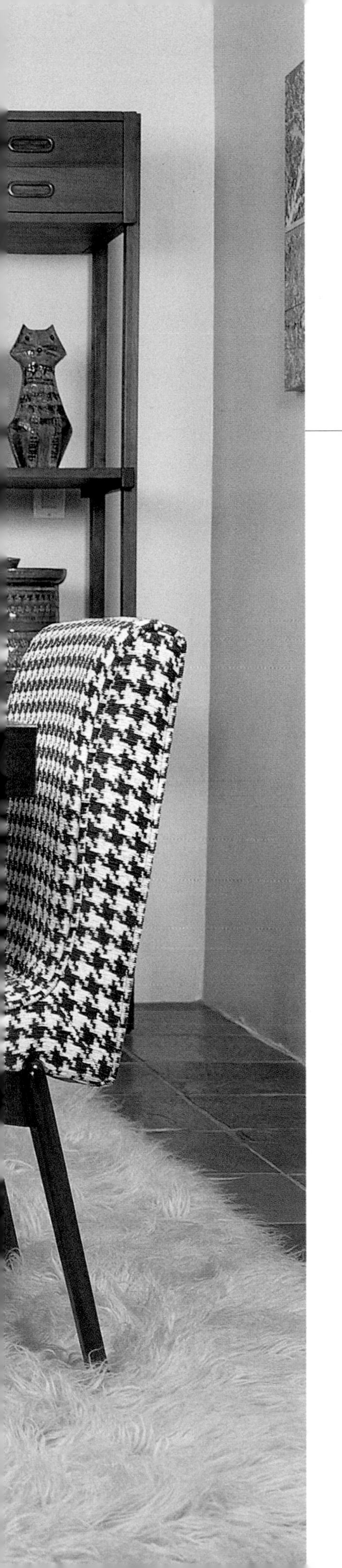

The Modernists

"WE WANTED something homey for me, yet masculine enough for Nick," says Carolyn Bernstein of the look she was after in the dining room of the '50s ranch house she shares with her husband, Nick Grad. And the couple didn't want to break the bank to get it. So they bought no-name midcentury furniture that needed a little TLC, gave it a lot, and got what they were looking for.

Check It Out

By buying vintage furniture that needed work, Grad and Bernstein saved a bundle. For $1,000 the couple scored a walnut dining table and six chairs (two not shown here). The pieces were dogs until the couple had them refinished and reupholstered in a practical, masculine wool with a brown-and-white houndstooth pattern. Sure, the restoration didn't come cheap—Grad and Bernstein spent $800 to have the work done—but the math still makes sense. A grand total of $1,800 divided by six chairs and a table equals about $200 or so per chair and $600 for the table. You'd be hard-pressed to find a full dining set (either a new or a perfectly restored vintage version) for less than three times that price. Even better, buying run-down pieces enabled the couple to customize them to reflect a family-friendly version of all things midcentury. The quirky check suits Bernstein's sensibility just fine. "I really wanted a room that was vibrant and fun," she says, "and I got it."

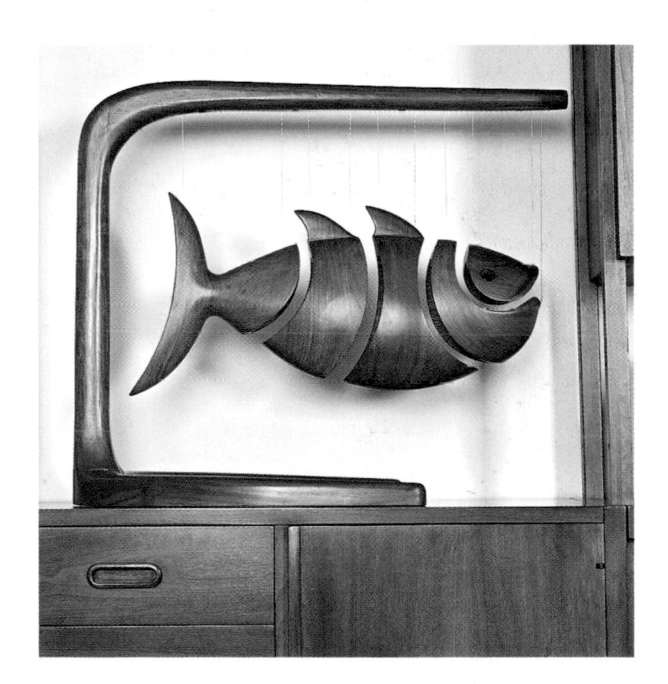

When should you spend the big bucks? Though it cost almost as much as their dining room table and chairs, this fish sculpture (crafted by Howdy Doody's marionette-maker) creates a big impact in the small room, one effect a splurge should always have.

To fill the kitchen wall—and cover an unsightly electric panel—Darren Ransdell whipped up a flame picture, using two canvases and acrylic paint. The cost of his artistic statement: less than $50.

KEEP WHAT YOU CAN, THEN MAKE THE UNSIGHTLY THINGS ATTRACTIVE.

The Makeover

LAURIE AND BRIAN MURPHY burned through big bucks trying to update the lackluster galley kitchen in their West Hollywood condo. Aiming for a quick fix, they sunk $4,000 into stainless steel appliances. But the gleaming pieces only emphasized the peeling vinyl, clunky cupboards, and Nixon-era tile. So they called on designer Darren Ransdell, who took the leftovers and cooked up something better. And guess what? It didn't cost a lot of dough.

Ransdell's Redo

Although it only measures 80 square feet, the Murphys' galley kitchen was directly in sight of the front door, so the couple couldn't put off refurbishing it forever. Enter designer Darren Ransdell, who transformed their space for less than $3,000. His mission began with the kitchen cabinets. Since replacing them would cost a bundle, Ransdell hid the plastic fronts and cheesy woodgrain trim with primer and paint. He then addressed the ceiling light fixture, replacing its grimy panels with cheap colorful Plexiglas panels (see page 75). Watching the budget, Ransdell left half the white tile countertops as is, capping only the most visible area with Chemetal faux-stainless steel laminate. Despite his devoted salvaging, some items were beyond help, like the worn vinyl floor, which Ransdell replaced for a song (see next page). Also on his to-go list was the color scheme, grays and dirty whites, which only underscored the room's blandness. Ransdell recommended visual heat for the kitchen, and the Murphys approved of his eye-popping choices: a Cheese Whiz orange for the cabinets and a paler tangerine for the ceiling and walls. That way, Ransdell says, "the whole room wouldn't look nuclear." Now the former eyesore is a gathering place. "I was afraid I might get sick of all that orange, but it lifts my spirits," Laurie Murphy says. "It wows people. I live here, and I'm wowed by it, too."

Kitchen stuck in the '70s? Budget still there, too? Pry up the floor, break out the paint, and install some Plexiglas.

Ground Level

Linoleum, the real deal made from linseed oil, doesn't come cheap—about $4 a square foot. And this nostalgia trip is high maintenance, to boot. Vinyl knockoffs, which can be found at Lowe's and Home Depot for less than $1 a square foot, may not deliver quite the same look, but they don't need pampering and are easy to cut, fit, and lay yourself. Step one is prying up the old stuff, which, in the Murphys' case, easily came loose since it was cut from a single roll. (Individually laid squares, a bit more challenging, can be lifted with a pry bar or scraper.) Ransdell calculated in advance how many one-foot-square tiles he'd need and how many he'd have to cut to fit—making sure to leave room for the stripes. Because the kitchen's concrete subfloor was slightly uneven, he filled the dips with a bonding compound. Then he spread on some specially formulated glue for vinyl tile, which goes down white and turns clear when it's ready to adhere. (Henry 430 Clear Pro, around $10 a gallon, is tried-and-true.) To keep the vinyl soft and pliable for easy handling, Ransdell had a heat gun on hand (the less powerful and cheaper models—just fine for this job—run between $25 and $35 at most hardware stores). Lastly, he applied a vinyl sealer to the finished floor to protect it against dirt and make it even easier to clean. Time-consuming? Yes, but worth the trouble. Professional installation would have tripled the price.

Curtains, right, made from two cotton panels (around $13 a pair from Ikea), a custom rod ($50), and a bunch of 50-cent key rings from a local hardware store keep the Murphys' dirty dishes out of sight.

Mondrian Moment

The Murphys were tired of turning a blind eye to the dingy plastic panels in the drop-ceiling light, so part of Ransdell's rescue mission was to redo them without running up a tab. He realized the arty promise of the grim fly-specked fluorescent fixture by swapping out its yellowed pieces for custom-cut colored Plexiglas. (Most plastics stores will cut to order.) In this case, the bars dividing the panels were already in place, so Ransdell was able to simply pop the new pieces in after painting the whole framework black. (Metal crossbars are available at Home Depot or any building-supply store.) At a total price of $100, the light now glows like a Mondrian painting.

Kitchens & Dining Seating

"A chair is a very difficult object to design. A skyscraper is almost easier," Mies van der Rohe once said. Were the legendary less-is-more architect alive today, he might be tempted to retract that statement—while sitting down in one of the dozens of well-designed chairs now available everywhere from Ikea and Target to Design Within Reach and West Elm. There's a style to suit every personality at prices that won't make you feel like the seat has been pulled out from under you. If you'd rather repair an old piece, check out the two totally different approaches in this chapter. Looking for a quick way to fix torn upholstery? Make a whimsical patch and put it on like a Band-Aid. Or stretch a piece of fabulous fabric over the seat and nail it on, upholstery style.

Mix It Up

We'll forgive you if you own a dining room suite, but only if you inherited it or won it on *The Price Is Right.* Not only do matched sets give a room that nauseating furniture-store feeling, but the cost is enough to make anyone queasy. A mix of pieces is far more interesting and easier to score for a song. Just ask interior designer Sasha Emerson, who found the '40s bamboo chairs, above, for only $75 each. "You never see cheap sets of eight," she says, "but it's easy to find four or fewer at good prices." She covered hers in a Carnaby Street–inspired chenille tapestry that coordinates with, but doesn't match, her other dining room chairs. If all your seats are identical, then pair them with a table of a different style. That's what Genifer Goodman did in her San Francisco dining room, left. The chairs are reproductions of the famed Emeco, bought for a shockingly low $25 each at a store closeout; the rough-hewn, stocky-legged table was once a store fixture. Goodman pulled it all together with a '60s tablecloth snagged at a flea market.

Design snob on a dime store budget? Check out the chic chairs that will run you just a little more than loose change.

1. RETRO

2. UPHOLSTERED

3. CONTEMPORARY CAFE

The Best Seats in the House

Forking over $400 for a dining room chair may seem like a perfectly fine idea—until it hits you that eating alone isn't much fun. Try adding five dinner companions and you're talking more than a couple thousand dollars. But that was then. In the past few years a new wave of talent has become intent on—you might even say obsessed with—getting low-priced, high-style seating into our homes. They've picked up the mantle of Charles and Ray Eames, who devoted themselves to producing smartly designed furniture priced for the masses some 50 years ago (when their chairs retailed for less than $20). The result has been a windfall of cheap, chic options from designers like Mario Bellini, Jasper Morrison, and Philippe Starck. Beyond that, a handful of savvy retailers are leading the charge, making these designs available far and wide. The chairs themselves come in all manner of shapes, styles, and materials; plastic seats are typically lower in price, but you can just as easily find great-looking, affordable chairs in metal, vinyl, and wood. Here are six styles that don't cost a fortune, even if you buy a complete set of six.

1. RETRO

Curvy chrome and sparkly vinyl make this diner chair flamboyantly fun in a '50s kind of way. We found it at Target for well under $100; you can also look for it

4. ARMCHAIR

5. FOLDING

6. INDUSTRIAL

at Kurt Petersen Furniture or restaurant-supply stores.

2. UPHOLSTERED

It's not your mother's fussy dining room chair by any stretch—except for the fabric pulled taut over its clean lines. At about half the price of a standard upholstered seat, West Elm's option adds a fashionista touch to any lair.

3. CONTEMPORARY CAFE

Bentwood chairs by German-born designer Thonet have nothing—except a big price tag—on these Asian beauties found in Kyoto's hip eateries. But Japan is a long way to go for a chair. Luckily the clean and classic beechwood seats are now sold stateside at Design Within Reach.

4. ARMCHAIR

What more could you want from Heller's ArcoBellini? Its brightly colored bold shape is comfortable indoors and out, and it stacks. You certainly can't say all that about the old-fashioned version.

5. FOLDING

Only in France would a seat so elegant be relegated to the outdoors. Here, the simple, classic design of Smith and Hawken's Parisian Park chair begs to be let in. Six will set you back about the price of discounted airfare to the City of Light. Splurge on a few more and fold them up until you need them. Find similar styles at flea markets and garden-supply stores.

6. INDUSTRIAL

Classroom chic? Homeroom decor? Elementary Eames? Whatever you call it, the simple design—and less-than-$50 price tag—of this desk chair from School Outfitters.com gets an A+.

What's the easiest way to rescue a ripped chair? Give it a patch job. A sleepy seat? Cover it with groovy fabric.

PROJECT:
HERE'S ONE YOU CAN NAIL DOWN FAST

If that vintage Pucci scarf is languishing in a drawer, perhaps you should apply it to your keister. According to L.A. designer Sasha Emerson, you can use any kind of fabric to reupholster a chair cushion, as long as you protect it with a layer of clear vinyl. To get started, measure your chair's seat, add a few extra inches to each side, and head to a craft store to buy enough one-inch-thick upholstery foam, batting, and eight-gauge clear vinyl to cover those dimensions. Then hit the hardware store for a can of Duro spray-on adhesive, a staple gun, and half-inch staples. First, unscrew the seat from the frame, pop off the staples that hold the old fabric in place, and toss the old foam. If your chair is as ho-hum as ours was, left, paint the frame with semigloss latex. Next, trim the new foam so that a quarter-inch strip hangs over each side of the unattached wooden seat. Spray both the seat and the foam with adhesive (open windows for ventilation), lay the foam on the seat, and place some heavy books on it to help it stick. After it dries, fold the foam's edges over to make a small hem and stretch it tightly under the seat. Have a friend hold the foam in place as you staple it at every inch. Stretch the batting, which keeps the fabric from eroding the foam, tightly over the foam, fold it under the seat, creating hospital corners, staple, and trim the excess. Repeat with your decorative fabric, then the vinyl. For an optional finishing touch, you can hammer upholstery tacks a quarter inch apart along the seat's edge. Finally, reattach the snazzy seat to the frame and give yourself a standing ovation. With a chair this hot, you won't want to sit down.

PROJECT: QUICK CHAIR REPAIR

Poor office chair. It probably spent the first half of its life in some stuffy corporate tower and the second half with stuffing protruding from its seat. As for the future? A sad array of gashes made this neglected baby, above, a likely candidate for the garbage dump—or worse, the expensive reupholsterer. Instead, we saved it with a little creative cut-and-paste action. How? First, take a piece of paper and draw circles, stripes, flowers, Matisse-inspired amorphous blobs, or any other design large enough to disguise your upholstered furniture's rips, cigarette burns, or red wine stains. Cut the designs out and lay them atop the piece to make sure they cover whatever it is you're trying to hide. Then trace these paper templates onto felt (for fabric upholstery) or vinyl (for leather) and cut them out. After that, it's as easy as pasting the designs onto the chair with a super-strong flexible glue, like Household Goop contact adhesive and sealant (about $4 at most hardware stores). Be patient and allow at least 24 hours for the stuff to dry. Otherwise, you'll risk getting glued to your seat.

Kitchen & Dining Details

You've spent a lot of time—and a chunk of change—on the perfect stove and fridge, so why does your kitchen look more like an appliance alley than a pleasant place to cook? Could be that those two hulking necessities are standing in the way of what makes the room truly yours. So, where do you begin? With your wastebasket, for starters. Just flip it over and hang it from above to make a cool pendant lamp. A colander works, too. Then seek out sophisticated shelves. You'll find that the sky's the limit on places to put your dishes—even if your budget's ceiling has dropped to an all-time low. Whether from industrial sources or chain stores, there's a sparkling solution to suit your space for much less than $100. If timeworn is to your taste, consider an old library cart. For warmth and character, it will always stack up.

Old Objects, New Tricks

In L.A. designer Sasha Emerson's East Coast summer house, almost everything was purchased at some kind of discount—then repaired, reupholstered, or simply assigned a new purpose. Her talent for using flea market and thrift shop finds in unexpected ways shows up all over her kitchen, where she put this old library cart ($75 from a vintage furniture shop), left, to work. As pretty as a still life painting, it holds her favorite cookbooks and a mix of vintage and new cake stands that she uses to hold fruits and vegetables. On the wall to the left of it, a secondhand chalkboard keeps track of phone messages. Above: A $5 flea market wine bucket may have once chilled great vintages, but Emerson prefers to use it as a catchall for cooking utensils on her countertop.

What do a wastebasket,
colander, bucket, and fish
trap have in common?
They've all seen the light.

The Kitchen Gets Cozy

Where some might give up the fight to salvage square footage and hang a Peg-Board in defeat, San Francisco interior designer Charles de Lisle retaliated, eking a whole extra room out of this small kitchen corner, right. Now he can relax in the '30s wing chair while the soup simmers. De Lisle swapped old pillows for this handsome piece at an upholsterer's shop and had it recovered with $200 worth of vintage Waverly cotton. "The large-scale pattern animates the traditional chair," he explains. A visit to the former home of the late architect Richard Neutra inspired the off-kilter arrangement of seascapes ($80 to $250 at antiques shops). Atop the bookshelves, a coil of rope becomes a sly objet d'art. But perhaps the most clever cash—and space—saver is the hanging lamp de Lisle improvised from a Balinese fish trap (a $5 swap meet steal) and a $10 yellow hardware-store chain.

1

2

Made in the Shade

Attach a hanging lamp-cord set (available at hardware stores, Ikea, and Pier One) to an ordinary household item, and you'll see it in an entirely different light.

1. TRASH LIGHT Flip a wicker wastebasket over and use wire cutters to clip a hole at the center of the bottom, just big enough for the socket to slip through.

2. HOLEY ILLUMINATION Enlarge one of the holes in the bottom of a colander using a heavy-duty drill and a titanium bit.

3

4

3. BRIGHTER SHADE OF PAIL Drill a hole in the center of the bottom of a metal bucket, then use tin snips to make the opening large enough for the cord to fit through.

4. POSTMODERN PLASTIC Unfold five construction bulb guards. Snap off the plastic clips, then attach the guards to one another at the top and bottom with plastic zip ties, and trim off any excess; affix the bulb socket to the new shade with floral wire. (Guards and zip ties are sold at stores like Lowe's and Home Depot.)

Open shelves are a savvy storage solution, especially the models that don't sap your money supply.

Buy Mass, Make It Yours

Designer Demi Adeniran makes use of every square inch of space in her kitchen, without creating visual clutter. In that often-overlooked stretch of wall between the countertop and cabinets, Adeniran found room to hang a smart dish drainer that functions as a handsome display shelf for her glassware, too. She found both the shiny rack and the stainless steel mounting strips at Ikea for under $30. The drinking glasses, which look like Venetian handblown tumblers, came from Crate and Barrel. In such sophisticated surroundings (she splurged on the the marble countertop), though, who would guess their humble origins?

Garnish and Serve

When designer Charles de Lisle moved into his Potrero Hill rental, the kitchen was at least clean, white, and basic; though, as de Lisle points out, it had "no work surfaces or useful storage whatsoever." Instead of installing built-ins, the designer made some simple, budget-savvy fast fixes.

For much-needed storage, de Lisle turned to restaurant-supply sources, where he found a $220 butcher-block-topped worktable and sturdy steel shelving that set him back $100 for six shelves and brackets. In addition to being affordable, the industrial pieces can change to fit his needs (add more brackets; move the table elsewhere) or travel with him to a new apartment. Plus, the exposed shelving keeps everything at hand and turns the dishware itself into wall decor.

De Lisle relies on a couple of common colors and doesn't sweat the mismatched sets, peppering his Crate and Barrel dishes with Ikea glasses and his own ceramicware.

"I love transforming things and finding new purposes for them....When you change something, you make it your own."

Great Crates

You can take the girl out of France... but you can't keep her from putting French wine crates to clever use when she's across the pond. In the kitchen of her Hollywood Hills home, designer Chantal Dussouchaud, above, turned wine crates from the Saint-Emilion region (near where she was born) into kitchen drawers. She suggests asking your local wine merchant if he will sell them to you—some may even offer them for free. Making the wooden boxes into clever storage is easy. Dussouchaud screwed four three-quarter-inch ball or roller casters on each crate. She fastened two casters to the front of the crates about four inches from the short side and one inch from the long side. The back casters are set just one inch from the short edge of the crate.

3

Rest assured, the ideas and projects in this chapter will inspire you to wake up and change your sleepy bedroom decor.

Bedrooms

You know the stats. We spend nearly a third of our lives doing it. But if sleep were all that happened in our bedrooms, then it wouldn't matter much what they look like. But everybody's got to open their eyes sometimes. If you're tired of waking up to drab surroundings, don't just hit the snooze button and hope for sweet oblivion. Take a look at the ways the gifted gang in this chapter have created stylish spaces for some serious relaxing, and you'll swear you're dreaming. When you learn that they all did it for peanuts, you'll pinch yourself. But it's true: A stapler and a bolt of burlap will cover cracked walls quicker than spackle, sandpaper, and paint. And a $5 rebar rod will hold up your curtains just as well as high-priced–and ho-hum–hardware. Collections cluttering up your closets? Pull them out of dusty storage and arrange them all over your bedroom walls (it's free). If it's the bed itself that bores you, stitch together a colorful quilt or a simple slipcover for the headboard. Or customize your dust ruffle. Can't stand the thought of starting up the sewing machine? Then simply change your sheets. Check out the smashing sets on pages 110 to 111. Other clever options include innovative side tables, ingenious storage solutions, and ways to display your personal mementos that will make you smile first thing every morning. So go ahead, give your bedroom a rousing wake-up call.

LARGE-SCALE PIECES CAN EXPAND SMALL ROOMS.

The Texturalist

"EVERY ROOM DESERVES a splurge," advises interior designer Charles de Lisle, "one big, bold statement to give it a kick in the pants." The totemic orange lamp in the bedroom of his tiny San Francisco cottage may scream big bucks, but the rest of the room is loaded with ingenious quick, cheap fixes, compliments of the local flea market—and his office stapler.

Bedroom Buys

When Charles de Lisle rented his 1940s cottage in Potrero Hill, the bedroom was so small and shoddy that even this fan of the forlorn found it hard to love. But with a little fabric and a few flea market finds, he satisfied his taste for texture and tranquility. Here's how:

1 ROUGH TREATMENT De Lisle banished bland paint and uneven woodwork by covering his bedroom walls with 48-inch raffia cloth purchased for $7 a yard. He stapled it directly onto the wall (using a run-of-the-mill office stapler) and frayed the edges. "I like the rawness," he notes. "It doesn't try to look too done." At $120 for the whole room, the raffia packs a dramatic punch without eating up any space (and comes down easily, a plus when your lease expires). "It's more expensive than paint," the designer says. "But it gives unexpected texture."

2 SPREAD IT ON The cotton bedspread, snatched up on sale for $100 at New York's ABC Carpet & Home, is still cheaper than a down comforter, and contrasts beautifully with the raffia's rough weave. Can't make it to Manhattan? Look for textured cotton spreads at your local Linens 'n Things.

3 HEAD OF THE CLASS Just because you don't have room for a king-size bed doesn't mean you can't have a king-size headboard. When de Lisle found this '40s beauty, attributed to Paul Laszlo, for $500 at a vintage store, he didn't hesitate. He simply placed it sideways, where it serves as a focal point and provides storage.

4 MIX MASTER De Lisle made the "Marlboro Man" collage out of plywood, part of an old billboard, wire, Hawaiian cocktail napkins, polyurethane, and nail polish.

5 DIAL UP The vintage Ericsson phone (the designer calls it his "Bat phone") was picked up for $50 at a trade show.

6 MODERN MOVEMENT Not everything in the bedroom is old. "It's important to celebrate the icons of today's design too," says de Lisle, who spent $450 on a Marcel Wanders orange lamp. "A mix of styles keeps things interesting."

7 FLOOR SHOW The wool rug is a $300 showroom sample from Specialty Textiles. But Pottery Barn, Ikea, and Crate and Barrel often have similar styles. Or look for unusual remnants, which you can have bound for very little money.

1
6
2
5
7

Metal, wood, and lucite frames, found at antiques malls for $5 to $20, hold a collection of family photos. On the mantle, Mary Catherine Lamb created a "personal altar" to her miniature mementos collected from around the world.

MORE IS LESS OF A MESS WHEN YOU ARRANGE SIMILAR OBJECTS IN GROUPS.

The Display Type

WHAT HAPPENS WHEN a quiltmaker with a painter's touch, a collector's soul, and an accountant's eye for the bottom line moves from a one-bedroom apartment to a 10-room American foursquare? For Mary Catherine Lamb, it was a chance to carefully curate her secondhand finds and create charming dioramas all over the house. Collecting wonderful and quirky objects is just the first step—Lamb's real genius is in coming up with ways to showcase her finds so that everyone can enjoy them.

All Together Now

If one sock monkey looks odd, how can 30 look so right? And if a single glove appears lonesome, how can more than 25 hang solo so stylishly? In the hands of Lamb, there's not only safety in numbers, but a captivating visual statement, too. A barrel of sock monkeys, captured at yard sales and flea markets for $3 to $12 each, lounges beneath the window of her bedroom, right and above. She created the colorful "valance" using ladies' gloves—in kidskin, leather, and silk—nabbed at estate sales for $1 to $5 a pair. Lamb notes that "singles are even cheaper." Opposite: She liberated her vintage print handkerchiefs from a drawer by hanging them as a colorful border. Double-sided tape has held them in place for 13 years.

Totally Tubular

A flat screen would be pretty as a picture hanging on your wall. But does the damage it could do to your wallet keep you lugging your ugly TV in and out of the closet to keep up appearances *and* satisfy your clicker craving? No longer. Feast your eyes on the lineup of sets available now. They're as mod as they are moderately priced. This Memorex 13-inch color television, above, is typical of the small, stylish new boob tubes that reference the past while incorporating all the latest technology. Or check out eBay for reconditioned classics from the '50s and '60s. Then you can proudly set your TV out for everyone to see. Rather fall asleep to sparkling flames than Seinfeld repeats? Turn that space-age TV into an old-fashioned hearth; Lagoon Games' instant fireplace video delivers 45 soothing minutes of crackling, sputtering flames.

EVEN A COMMITTED MINIMALIST CAN USE COLOR TO THE MAX.

The Unlikely Colorist

"I HAVE A THING FOR ORANGE," admits Demi Adeniran. But when it came to her bedroom, the interior designer was looking for tranquility. So she compromised with a sea of white—linens, lamp shades, walls—punctuated by small hits of her favorite shade. While the hue isn't subtle, the placement of it is; there's just enough to add zing without disturbing the peace.

Room to Rest

Adeniran created calm in her tiny bedroom by putting everything in its place. How? She installed a birch plywood storage cabinet beneath the windows, left, that practically disappears into the wall. Thanks to tufted cushions covered in beige mohair, it does double duty as a window seat. In between, she set an orange-painted plywood platform sized to lift her tiny television just high enough to make watching from bed comfortable. Right: When she bought her apartment, the bedroom closets sported traditional doors that swung out and took up too much space. So she replaced them with crisp curtains. In addition to moving back and forth on a hospital track, they give the illusion of windows where none exist.

A bouquet of roses is nature's nod to Demi Adeniran's color scheme. The bright arrangement adds pizzazz without overwhelming.

PROJECT:
GIVE YOUR HEAD-BOARD THE SLIP

When Adeniran grew tired of the French country style that had been her passion, she couldn't afford all new furniture. So rather than pitch her ornately carved headboard, above, she sewed a white slipcover for it—which also proved a better foil for the graphic lines of her beloved antique Chinese side tables. "I also have another slipcover with bright orange trim," she says, "for when I get bored." Here's how to make a simpler version. Use heavy-weight fabric for an instant upholstered look like this. Wash the fabric to preshrink it. Trace the headboard's outline on a piece of kraft paper. Add two inches all around the perimeter (more if the headboard is especially thick), and cut out a template. Pin the pattern to a double layer of fabric and cut out. With right sides facing, sew the two pieces together, with a half-inch seam. Double-turn the bottom half inch to the reverse; press and stitch. Turn right side out and slide the cover over the headboard.

A tailored dust ruffle adds clean lines—and extra storage. But you don't have to settle for standard-issue.

Style—From the Ground Up

To give her bedroom a potent punch of color, Adeniran began at the bottom by crafting a graphic border for her dust ruffle, right. She made the bed skirt herself, but it's easy to replicate the look with any standard white dust ruffle (Wal-Mart, Target, and Kmart offer versions for less than $30). Just stitch a two-inch-wide strip of colorful fabric—or, for a more feminine look, a series of grosgrain ribbons—along the hem. A bright orange throw picks up where the colorful perimeter leaves off, infusing the room with just enough dramatic color to have an impact. Adeniran dressed her bed in white linens, transforming it into a model of modernity by covering the headboard in a slipcover she made herself (see instructions, opposite).

Sew chic: Trimmed with bold color, a white bed skirt goes from plain to punchy with just a few stitches on the sewing machine.

ALAMEDA FREE LIBRARY

NUIT
LEKKER
Z... Z... Z... z...

IT'S SIMPLE TO MAKE PLAIN JANE SNAPPY WITH SCISSORS AND A SEWING MACHINE.

The Customizer

CHANTAL DUSSOUCHAUD may be an expert with a sewing machine, but that doesn't mean she wants to do everything herself. She understands that great pieces are available at great prices. For her Hollywood Hills bedroom, she took a store-bought duvet, then added her personal touch. That way she didn't have to spend a fortune—or days of work—to get a custom, one-of-a-kind look.

And Sew to Bed

An experienced seamstress like Chantal Dussouchaud isn't above using mass-manufactured bed linens. By tacking a luxurious piece of linen onto a plain white cotton duvet, she gave the basic a lot of cachet for just a little cash. How? She bought the quilt cover at Ikea (Bed Bath & Beyond, Kmart, and Sears offer similar styles) and sewed oversize buttons and finely woven tan linen to its bottom half. The playful look doesn't stop at the foot of the bed; there's a bit of pillow talk going on as well. Dussouchaud stenciled a phrase in French, her native tongue, and one in Dutch, her husband's, on boudoir pillows using stencil letters and fabric paint. *Bonne nuit* ("good night"), *slaap lekker* ("sleep well"), and the universally understood expression for snoozing send them to bed each night. "My pillow collection is a reaction against the shortening of vocabulary in our daily lives," the designer explains. She may be savvy with the soft goods, but Dussouchaud doesn't go in for high-priced hardware, either. She kept the cost of the two-tone curtains down by sewing them herself, then hung them from a $5 rebar rod. With so many handcrafted pieces, the room could easily look a bit down-home, but by limiting the color palette to neutrals on a bold black background, Dussouchaud achieved a graphic yet graceful effect.

Plain closet doors became a French country focal point in the guest bedroom after Chantal Dussouchaud knocked out their upper panels and replaced them with chicken wire. She then hung a pair of curtain rods on the inside of each door and stretched batik fabric between them.

RUMMAGE THROUGH THE REMNANT BIN FOR THE REAL DEALS.

The Restorer

GIVE SASHA EMERSON a piece of old fabric and she'll return the favor with a fabulous quilt, a funny framed piece, or a fanciful upholstered chair. So, for this L.A.–based interior designer, the remnant bin was naturally the first place to turn when she wanted to transform a bland bedroom into a colorful style statement that her little girls would love.

A graphic fabric remnant, $1 a yard, updates an office chair, above, unearthed for $22 at a used-furniture store. Sasha Emerson's parents brought the poster back from China: She had it matted in panda bear shirt fabric and framed in faux bamboo.

Three's a Charm

I grew up with a father who never passed a yard sale without stopping and a mother who could add a piece of velvet to an old blazer and turn it into something beautiful," recalls Sasha Emerson. One look around the bedroom she created for her daughters and you see the power of genetics at work. With twin beds, two are expected, three are fresh—and practical for a woman with three girls. Emerson paid $150 each for the midcentury Paul Frankl frames at Futurama, a favorite vintage store in L.A, then spent $225 to have them all refurbished. Instead of buying perfectly preserved quilts, she found unfinished quilt tops, $5 to $10 each at a flea market, bought some batting, and paid a seamstress to sew them all together.

Going to Pieces

If you find an old quilt for under $100, consider yourself lucky. A vintage quilt in good condition, even one of no historical importance, often runs anywhere from $500 to $1000. (And just try pricing an Amish beauty.) According to Emerson, even worn, ripped ones can cost up to $50. So she suggests looking for small quilt pieces or quilt fronts without backing (she finds hers through a textile dealer at her local flea market). You can hire a seamstress to stitch the pieces together and apply cotton batting and backing. Depending upon the amount of work needed, it may cost anywhere from $80 to $200, but you're still likely to come out ahead pricewise. And don't pass up worn beauties. Often these can be repaired easily. "When I spot a quilt with a big rip in it, I see it as a virtue," says Emerson.

IT'S SO MUCH EASIER TO MAKE UP A BED WHEN YOU CAN WALK AROUND IT.

The Space Conquerer

WHEN ARCHITECT Stephen Atkinson designed a 550-square-foot house for his parents John and Brenda in rural Louisiana, he knew that furnishing the small place would be a big challenge. So he created pieces that are scaled to the size of the rooms and do double duty. In the bedroom, the center becomes the focus—and things are not necessarily what they seem.

Free-Floating

Stephen Atkinson not only worked his money-saving magic on the construction of his parents' corrugated metal country retreat (the D.I.Y. dream house cost $41,000 to build), he lent his savvy sleight of hand to furnishing the place, too. In the tiny bedroom—it's 11 by 12 feet—Atkinson pulled what seems like serious extra square footage out of his hat by using a few of his favorite design tricks. By plunking the bed down in the middle of the room he created drama—and space to walk around. He designed the platform bed with a built-in headboard that hides a bookcase and provides a resting place for reading lamps, eliminating the need for side tables. He also installed floor-to-ceiling doors at the foot of the bed (any shorter and they would have given the space a decidedly suburban feel), which open the room to the great outdoors. Now that's really fooling Mother Nature.

What looks like a bedspread and drapes like one, too? A tablecloth, of course. This one was around $20 at Ikea.

DICTIONARY of CULTURAL LITERACY
PHILOSOPHY
THE CALL OF THE WILD
THE HEROES
PAUL BUNYAN
MERRY ADVENTURES OF ROBIN HOOD
YOUNG PEOPLE'S SCIENCE ENCYCLOPEDIA
UNITED STATES NAVAL RESERVE
HISTORY OF ART · H.W. JANSON

Bedroom Details

Sure, the bed may be the biggest item, but that doesn't mean there aren't plenty of other opportunities to add excitement to your bedroom. What about the walls? One couple put a peg rail 'round the room and switch between paintings, pretty antique dresses, and precious kids' artwork. An intrepid yard saler scored a collage of champagne corks and put the "pop" art over his bed. Even side tables are fair game for expressing a bit of off-beat flair. A piece of vintage luggage, with the addition of legs, can serve both as storage and a surface for holding a lamp, alarm clock, and books. And don't overlook less obvious options: A sinewy silver stool, a colorful square chair, or a retro TV tray may be just what your sleepy bedroom needs to wake it up.

Frame it Up

You don't need an art collector's budget to make a big impact on your walls. Just ask Carolyn Bernstein, who painted the self-portrait, left, when she had little more than lunch money in her pocket. The schoolgirl painting makes the grade because Bernstein gave it the gallery treatment with an elegant linen mat and wood frame. Homegrown art always works, even if it doesn't come from your own hands. Genifer Goodman prefers paint-by-numbers on her walls, particularly of horses, like the one that hangs over her bed, above. "I'm not an equestrian, but I was drawn to the colors and composition of this one," says Goodman. "It's not perfect or meticulous, and it's loaded with personality." She never pays more than $25 for the paintings, which she now finds primarily on eBay rather than at fleas. "Once I got on the horse kick, it was fun to look at all the options online."

Are boring white bed linens
causing you to snore?
Try some of these patterned
picks on for sighs.

Dream Themes

A perfect pair of hips isn't the only place to hang a happening hula skirt these days. Dress a bed in tikiwear, opposite, and dream of your own fantasy island. This tropical sleeper is only a snip away, thanks to a few raffia table skirts (we snagged these from OrientalTrading.com) trimmed to standard dust ruffle length and attached to the top of a box spring with a few dozen T-pins. Completing the luau look: Pottery Barn's beachy-keen duvet cover and pillow shams. If wild horses couldn't get you to wear those skirts, then go in for a little paddock panache: Get the cool cowpoke look, above, by slapping a herd of Wallies' vinyl-coated stallions (around $20 for a three-horse set) above a nest feathered with Garnet Hill's natty pony and polka-dot linens. Too tame for you? Jonathan Horowitz and Rob Pruitt used bargain satin sheets from Bed Bath & Beyond, a dirt cheap grandfather clock fitted out with battery-operated guts, and Horowitz's silk-screened pillowcases to create a macabre mood.

Make your own bedroom table with a little bit of loot and a lot of style on the side.

Lost Luggage?

What do you get when you combine a battered old suitcase and a shapely set of legs? A storage unit–cum–side table like the one at right. If your luggage is in good condition, you're already a step ahead. This suitcase had fallen on hard times, so we covered all of its silver details with masking tape and painted on a couple of coats of high-gloss latex in robin's egg blue. Don't have short table legs lying around? Ikea sells them for around $15 for four, or check out Home Depot or your local hardware store. Simply turn the suitcase upside down and measure an equal distance from each corner, using a pencil to mark the spots. Then drill or poke a small hole at each mark. From there, it depends on the hardware that comes with your table legs. Most can be screwed into the bottom of the suitcase and secured with a bolt on the inside. Once you get the legs on, start packing. Fill it with blankets and pillowcases, close it up, and set a lamp on top.

Show Your Stripes

Make this swanky striped table, right, the way New York decorator Christopher Coleman did. He cleaned the surface of a plain table and stuck on tape in a variety of colors and widths. No sanding, painting, or refinishing required. Coleman found his bold-hued tape on eBay (a couple of batches totalled around $60) by typing *electrical tape* and *packing tape* into the addictive auction site's search engine. But you can also head down to your local hardware store to case out its selection. If you're lucky, you'll get the same reaction Coleman got. "It's sensational," he says. "People can't believe it!"

When is a side table not a side table? When it's a shapely stool, a stubby stump, or a simple chair.

1. COOL CUBE

2. SLEEK STOOL

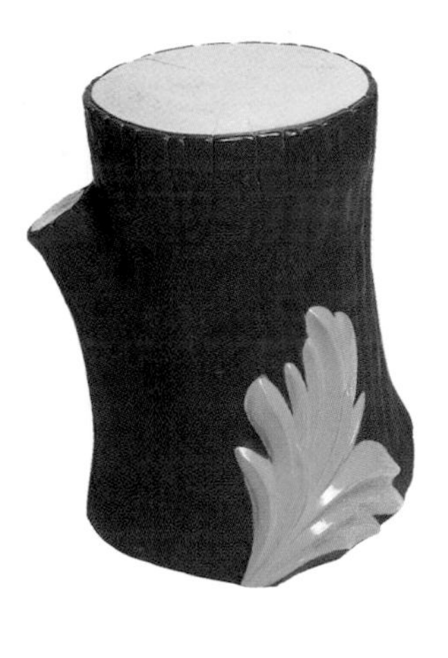

3. STARCK'S STUMP

Try These on for Sides

If the perfect bedside table is still a figment of your imagination, perhaps you've been looking in all the wrong (i.e., expected) places. Forget typical versions; they'll just make your room look, well, typical. Instead, take a look at the pieces we would put in our pads. They're all around $200 or less, so they'll only stretch your imagination, not your budget.

1. COOL CUBE

Since when do side tables have to sit on the floor? This wall-mounted model frees up space so that you can squeeze that queen-size mattress into your twin-size lair. If you've got room to roam, stack 'em two high on the floor. These from West Elm cost approximately $180 for a set of four; both Crate and Barrel and PBteen often have similar pieces.

2. SLEEK STOOL

Sure this cool, curvaceous creature makes anyone sitting on it more beautiful, but picture the piece beside your high-rise bed and you'll hope it never sees another backside. The sleek aluminum 30-incher from Pure Design Classics may seem steep at around $200, but it stands up to the design snob in all of us—and it's sturdy, too.

3. STARCK'S STUMP

When Philippe Starck unveiled his collection of quirky outdoor gnome stools/tables/conversation pieces for Kartell in 1999, the little guys got all the attention, and this simple accom-

4. VINTAGE TV TRAY

5. SIDE CHAIR

6. GARBAGE PAIL

panying stump was overlooked. Now the bearded imps are getting tired, but this hand-painted plastic piece seems as fresh and woodsy as ever. The Saint Esprit stool-table delivers that forest feeling for just under $200.

4. VINTAGE TV TRAY

They've been around since the eighteenth century, but it wasn't until television—and the advent of Swanson entrées in the 1950s—that lightweight folding tables became a staple in nearly every American household. They were designed for eating and watching, but are often good-looking and solid enough to serve as permanent side tables, too. We found this vintage print of spindles, weather vanes, and gas lamps on eBay, where a set of four cost a mere $50.

5. SIDE CHAIR

With lines this clean and simple, the dining room essential can sidle easily up to a bed. The perfectly flat seat of this chair (it's the Edvard from Ikea and goes for approximately $40) is begging for a stack of books; its level surface will keep your water in the glass and within arm's reach. And it can be painted (and re-painted) any color to mix or match with your bedroom decor.

6. GARBAGE PAIL

The flip side of a trash can gives a room just the right tossed-off look while keeping you right on budget. This lacquered steel model from Ikea costs around $15; or shell out a few more bucks and you can get a flat-topped version from Martha Stewart's tony catalog.

Go shopping in your own house for original art. A pretty robe, a nifty necklace, or art made by tiny hands can be as prized as a masterpiece.

Clothes Encounters

When guests stay at Jolie Kelter and Michael Malcé's 1890s farmhouse on Long Island's East End, they are treated to an intimate view of the couple's quirky collecting spirit. To make up for the absence of closets in the guest room, Malcé installed a simple—and super cheap—peg rail around the entire room, opposite. Inspired by the Shakers, he set the rail almost flush with the top window casing, making it the perfect height for hanging paintings, children's artwork, vintage dresses, and guests' clothing, too. Malcé nailed 1-by-4s to the wall, drilled holes at regular intervals, and pushed in wooden pegs, available at most hardware stores. If you're lucky enough to have closets, but not enough of them, pull out your prettiest clothing and pin it to the wall. The fanciful kimono-style robe, right, is a work of art itself; suspended from a sweet slip of pink grosgrain ribbon and secured to the wall with a simple white thumbtack, it can hang with the most expensive of 'em.

If sleepless nights are going to have you staring at the walls, at least make sure they're entertaining.

The Third Dimension

How fitting that collector Chip Cordelli scored the POP wall hanging, opposite, for 10 bucks at an estate sale just down the road from Andy Warhol's cliffside house in Montauk, Long Island. It's the kind of modern folk art Cordelli craves: recycled, innovative, and peppy. It's anyone's guess how the piece came to be, but Cordelli lets his imagination wander: Was it the result of a bag of champagne corks collected from years of parties, a lazy day with nothing else to do but run the jigsaw in a circle, and a big bottle of Elmer's glue? Why not? Your version could be. Left: Give your walls the fairest—and easiest—3-D treatment of all. Allen and Paulette Hoggatt hung two vintage mirrors on the wall in the guest room of their Louisiana lake house and used them to frame their favorite funny masks. The couple suspended the masks with transparent fishing line attached to metal hooks atop the frame. The result? They reflect the kind of personal style that money just can't buy.

POP

Own more than two of anything? Hang them up on your bedroom walls and call 'em your art collection.

Getting Personal

Family photos and quirky collections always make a bedroom more intimate, especially if you artfully arrange them on the wall. When Allen and Paulette Hoggatt had the chance to buy the lake house that had been in their family since 1946, they got a little something extra: generations worth of photographs and mementos accumulated by deeply talented relatives. Antiques dealers, hunters, and fly fishermen all passed through the doors at one time or another, leaving behind charming evidence of their passions. "There was great stuff everywhere," says Paulette, "but it took our cousin James, an artist and antiques dealer, to pull it all together." Here, he grouped a prize catch, a cork-lined shadow box displaying ties from the family fly fisherman, and decades worth of black-and-white snapshots. The deer hoof lamp came compliments of Uncle Thomas; he wanted a memento from his first successful hunt back in the 1930s.

Off the Wall

By the looks of their bedroom walls, the Kelter-Malcé marriage is a love match. Not only do Jolie and Michael share a passion for perusing antiques shops near their Long Island home and auctions farther afield, but they both love the off-beat objects that make their old farmhouse a wonder to wander around in. Someone with less confidence wouldn't dream of hanging hearts—one the size of a shop sign. "The giant tin heart is nice and rusty," says Malcé, "so it doesn't give the room that saccharin look." It's offset by a Victorian cushion, a plush velvet tufted chair, and an embroidered felt table skirt (all from auctions and antiques shops). Above: Downstairs, you'll find a bunch of bathing beauties in one corner. Inspired by Kelter's passion for swimming, the couple bought the amateur paintings whenever they found them, then placed an old smoking stand nearby to keep them company. They found the bathing cap display (with caps!) in their favorite antiques store.

4

Paper the walls, put up a punchy shower curtain, or spray-paint over a stained carpet. There are plenty of ways to redo the loo without taking a bath.

Bathrooms

It's usually one of the tiniest rooms in your house, so why does transforming your bathroom invariably end up being one of the most expensive projects? Fortunately, it doesn't have to be. Just look at how much style one woman has managed to cram into a few square feet, opposite. Demi Adeniran used inexpensive subway tiles ($4 a square foot), a flea market chandelier, and a standard $129 Formica vanity that she faced with beveled mirrors and topped with marble. Then, with just one grand gesture–she sewed the dramatic scarlet velvet shower curtain herself–she gave the room a final jolt of Hollywood pizzazz. Can't see going this glam? The designer on page 126 created a spot-on serene space (thanks to a can of spray paint and an eye for language) where there were once permanent stains. If you'd rather relax in a room full of your favorite furnishings, take your cues from the couple on page 130; they see no reason to resort to generic white porcelain. Another stylist signed a lease despite the gaping hole in his bathroom ceiling. It remains there 13 years later, because rather than foot the bill for a repair, he made a virtue of the unsightly opening; he hid it with a long tree branch that seems to be growing into the room, a solution that, like so many of the ones in this chapter, is as high impact as it is low budget.

DON'T DITCH THAT RUG: A CLEVER COVER-UP CAN SAVE A CRUMMY CARPET.

The Wordsmith

AS SOMEONE FLUENT in French, Italian, German, and English, interior designer Chantal Dussouchaud can't help herself. Her love of language, on view all over her Hollywood Hills home, gives the place a certain je ne sais quoi. Though you might not see the writing on the walls in her bathroom, you'll get a quick vocabulary lesson from the carpet on the floor. *Très chic, n'est-ce pas?*

Water, water everywhere: Clever use of spray paint (and various words for water) hides dark stains on the bathroom rug.

Out, Damned Spot

Your instincts may tell you to toss that carpet with one too many spills, but before you start ripping it up, consider how Dussouchaud resuscitated her bathroom's stained wool wall-to-wall, saving the rug from the trash bin. How did she do it? Dussouchaud marked off two stripes with masking tape, covered the rest of the floor in newspaper, and sprayed the exposed areas with brown Rust-Oleum. Next, she removed just enough paper to place letter stencils over the rug's stains. She sprayed those, too, and the carpet stayed put. You don't have to stick to words—try a grid, a checkerboard, even polka dots.

WATER

A BATHROOM IS A GOOD PLACE TO CLEAN UP, BUT IT DOESN'T HAVE TO BE STERILE.

The Gleaner

THE HOLE IN THE CEILING of Chip Cordelli's bathroom would have intimidated almost anyone. But undeterred, the stylist used ingenuity rather than plaster to cover it up. He simply stuck a tree branch into it, scavenged for shelving and cedar to cover stained walls, painted the place coral pink, then hung his flea market finds high and low to turn an eyesore into an eyepopper.

Salvage Style

Only a visionary with a knack for eccentric solutions could see the promise in such dilapidated digs. Here's what Cordelli did to redo his rental.

1 BRANCHING IN A leak in the apartment above had rotted the rafters and peeled away the paint from the Victorian tin ceiling. Cordelli made the resulting hole part of the scenery by wedging a tree branch he found on the street into it. He propped another branch in the corner next to the sink, right, to continue the theme.

2 THE BIG COVER-UP Rather than cough up his own cash to repair the rental's water-stained wall, Cordelli took inspiration (it's free) from the cedar woodwork of '60s and '70s beach houses. He gathered scrap cedar strips from a lumberyard and nailed them willy-nilly to the wall. "Now my bathroom smells like a sauna and makes me look like a real D.I.Y.er all at once," he says with a laugh.

3 STOLEN STORAGE Well, practically. The metal shelving is from Ikea, but the rest of the storage is made from scrap. Cordelli built the wall-mounted cabinet using medium-density fiberboard (MDF) he found in the cast-off bin at a lumberyard. A cheap alternative to wood, it's easy to cut, and its smooth surface is super paint-friendly. The wine crates that hold his books and medical bag came compliments of a wine warehouse.

Chip Cordelli's superb scavenging skills lead him to flea market finds most would overlook, like the plaster bust and wooden shoe form that hang over the medicine cabinet.

4 SOMETHING BLUE Cordelli kept the blue metal cabinet (it's office furniture) that came with the place. He uses the left side for a hamper and the right for storing toiletries and towels.

5 ON THE WALL Set against pink walls (Ralph Lauren Coral, $25 a gallon) is just a tiny fraction of Cordelli's quirky collections. He bought the THINK sign—an old IBM employee handout—at a yard sale 15 years ago; the anchor came from the nightclub his father owned for 30 years. The tennis racket clock is pure pool house chic. "In my world, the pool house *is* the bathroom."

1
2
3
4
ACQUA DI PARMA
HANDYMAN'S BOOK
THE DESIRE OF MY EYES
Labyrinths OF IRON
Doing Time
HAIR SPRAY

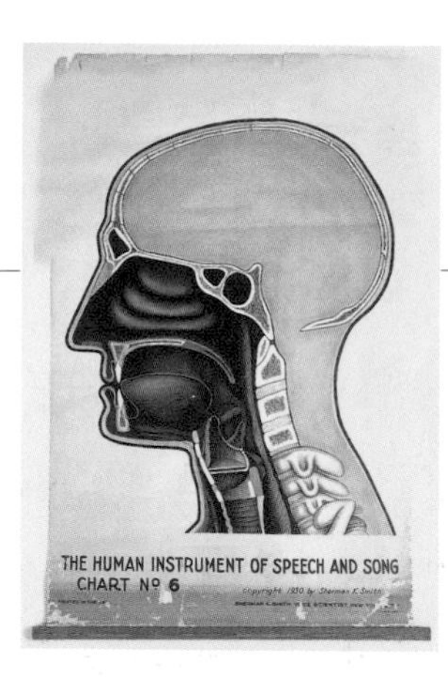

The Power of the Gory

Nothing endows a room with a more august (and slightly dusty) sense of the past than old science posters, such as the animal charts in the bathroom of Peacock Hill, or the 1930 vocal chart by Sherman K. Smith, above. Evocative of both seventh-grade science labs and evil-doctor horror flicks, vintage anatomy posters are an unlikely meld of sincerity and irony. If the prospect of pinning one to your wall makes your heart pound, keep in mind that some have better resale value than others. The most desirable works are by Peter Bachin, Frank Netter, and the early master Max Broedel. While quality vintage posters can be difficult to find on online auction sites, two New York City boutiques, Evolution and B-4 It Was Cool, carry a wide assortment.

NOT EVERY BATHROOM HAS TO BE TILED FROM TOP TO BOTTOM.

The Time Travelers

WHEN ROB PRUITT and Jonathan Horowitz were furnishing their 1895 mansion in upstate New York, they were inspired by the "Victorian notion of the world traveler, the scientist-collector with his cabinet of wonders," says Pruitt. Why not apply the same approach to the bathroom, too? Despite the array of unlikely objects, the redesign left them flush with cash.

Room to Relax

At Peacock Hill, Pruitt and Horowitz furnished the loo as lushly as any living room, working in a classical bust, a black lacquered chest for storage, and a green ceiling-bulb cover as objet d'art. Even the walls are well-appointed, with eerie educational posters from China, set in cheap poster frames. Wainscoting always gives a space a furnished feeling. The warm wood was there when the pair bought the place, but installing it new costs about one-fourth the price of tiling the walls. The couple left no surface unconsidered; they gussied up the exterior of the claw-foot tub (as well as its toe-nails) with black gloss paint and gave the toilet, right, the beauty treatment, too.

The toilet seat was just sitting there, bare, until Rob Pruitt and Jonathan Horowitz gave it the house imprimatur with a home-designed sticker (around $20 to print at a sign shop).

MAKE AT LEAST ONE BIG GESTURE IN A SMALL BATHROOM TO GIVE IT CHARACTER.

The Petite Retreat

THERE'S NOT MUCH ROOM to move, let alone redesign, in Charles de Lisle's tiny bathroom. But the intrepid interior decorator didn't let that stop him. What the space lacks in square footage, de Lisle makes up for in layers of richness and detail. By wrapping elegant fabric around the stark white washbasin, changing a lightbulb, pinning plants to the wall (a boon for black thumbs), and tossing quirky impulse buys into the mix, he has given the once-bland bathroom a luxurious look for less than $300.

Skirting the Issue

A piece of fabric takes up little if any space, so de Lisle looked to tune up his sink with an elegant, tailored skirt of Fortuny-style printed cotton, opposite. "This one yard of glamorous-looking fabric instantly gives the room a sense of style—and it hides the pipes, too," says the designer, who sewed the French-pleated skirt himself, then fastened it to the underside of the sink with a pair of Velcro strips. Above left: Since there was no space for potted plants, de Lisle attached small bromeliads to the wall with pushpins. "They only require a quick misting once a week," he promises. A vintage-style bulb ($68 from Rejuvenation) revives an existing fixture; a knotted rope adds a burst of texture and nautical appeal. Above right: Why Godzilla? De Lisle picked up the plastic toy on a whim in San Francisco's Japantown, and though that's how many of his collections began, he swears it's not the start of a new obsession.

Bathroom Details

Giving your bathroom a makeover doesn't mean you have to resort to an all-out face-lift; just give it a facial and stash the cash you save for something that will *really* change your life. By switching the shower curtain, repainting the walls, or simply sewing a bit of trim onto basic towels, you can lift your bathroom's spirits without spending a small fortune. Are your walls bland? Rather than live with plain white, go bold and bright, no matter how small your space (see the bubble gum pink bathroom on page 138). If you're looking for a D.I.Y. project, take inspiration from the room on page 139 and paper your walls with hundreds of strips from glossy magazine pages. Too time-consuming? In just an hour, you can tell it like it is by etching whatever statement you want on a water glass.

Reaching New Heights

Offbeat? Or elegant? A private space like your bathroom says a lot about you, so don't shirk the details. Whichever way you lean, carry your style through the whole room. Take the outstretched hand, above, by Propaganda, for example. This deliciously designed tub stopper is a winking way to express your sense of bathroom humor. And at around $8, it won't leave you drowning in debt. Left: If you prefer rooms that are more politely appointed, take inspiration from interior designer Chantal Dussouchaud. She rescued an old wood frame from a friend's garbage bin, spray-painted it, and then fitted it with a mirror. Peer into the glass and you see not one, but two shower curtains framing the tub like a window, complete with tiebacks fashioned from nautical rope.

Turn a plain $2 tumbler into a commanding thirst quencher in less than half an hour.

PROJECT:

MAKE YOUR ETCH A SKETCH

Who needs fancy crystal—or worse, ugly plastic—to hold toothbrushes or cotton balls? A mere $6.50 for a jar of etching cream, and any plain glass container can become a witty bathroom statement. The cream contains heavy-duty chemicals, so wear rubber gloves and work on a protected surface near running water in a well-ventilated area.

1. *Place a strip of masking tape on the outside of the glass so that the top of the tape aligns with the glass's lip.*
2. *Apply vinyl press-on letters.*
3. *Mask off the sides and bottom edge of the area to etch with three more strips of tape. Keep an even space around letters.*
4. *Stir the cream, then use a craft brush to paint an even, but fairly thick, coat within the taped-off rectangle. Leave on for five to 10 minutes.*
5. *Rinse thoroughly.*
6. *Gently remove the tape and letters, and hand wash the glass with dishwashing liquid. When it dries, you'll find your messages clearly spelled out.*

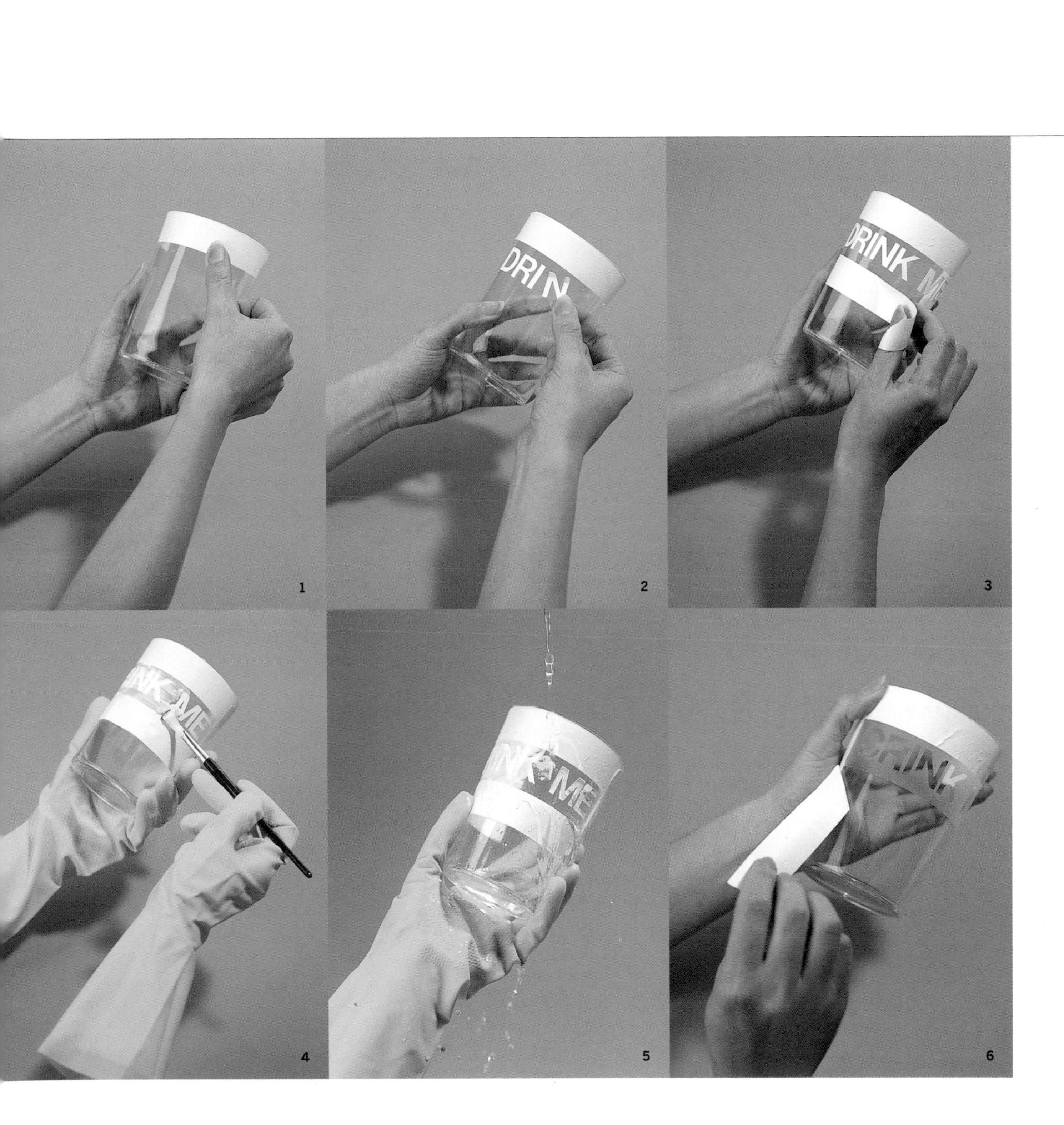
DRIN
DRINK ME
DRINK

No budget for a bathroom redo? Set your sights—and focus your effort—on creating a beautiful backdrop.

Pretty in Pink

If that box of Mr. Bubble brings back blissful childhood memories, why not put that pink on your bathroom walls to perk up the place? Sure, pure white might make this tiny 26-square-foot space seem roomier, but it could never give it the big personality that a wash of shocking color—here Benjamin Moore's Bubble Bath—does. Not only is it the least expensive way to make a grand gesture in such a small room, but it takes the pressure off the no-frills fixtures: a standard home-center toilet, sink vanity, and mirror. Delivering the style message falls to the walls and a few choice, cheap touches. Extrawide rickrack turns plain white Ikea towels into eye-catchers, and a 1960s pink hair dryer ($10 on eBay—and it works) does double duty as sculpture. Other vintage finds around the sink, including a Minnesota state tourism glass that holds toothbrushes, prove that funky can also be functional.

Shredded Bliss

If you've amassed more magazines than you can live with, take 'em to the shredder—and leave a paper trail framing the toilet. To create wall art from your bathroom reading, forage through those piles of periodicals and tear out the photo pages. Feel free to add other pretty pulp—fiction or otherwise—to the mix. Old maps, comic books, and gift wrap deliver miles of multicolored style. Next, find a shredder that makes strip, as opposed to cross, cuts (Staples sells one for around $15), and feed it your colorful concoction. Slice more than you'll need, then use the pieces that best suit your palette. Using a narrow paintbrush, apply a craft glue like Delta Sobo (four ounces for $2 at www.dickblick.com) to the backs of the paper strips. Place them in a pattern on a smooth, clean wall and allow them to set overnight. The next morning, brush on an even coat of transparent sealant (such as Minwax Polycrylic, available at Home Depot). Let it dry overnight, then soak up the view from your tub.

Here's one of the easiest ways to banish the bathroom blues without getting soaked.

1.
THE NEW SOPHISTICATE

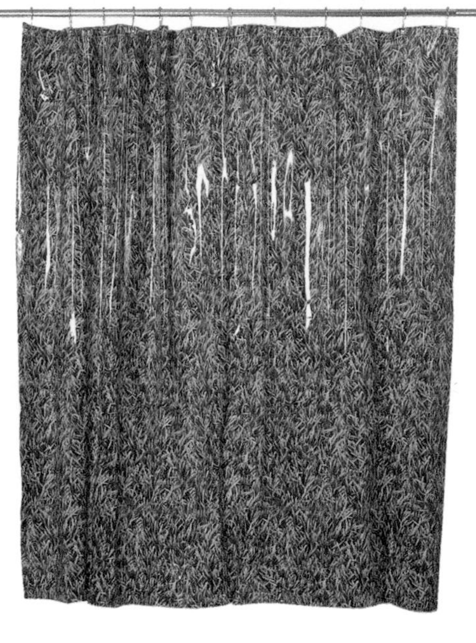

2.
THE ENVIRONMENTALIST

3.
THE SOLID CITIZEN

Curtain Call

It probably wouldn't fly with a clinical psychologist, but there are those who believe that a person's choice of shower curtain offers more insight into his or her personality than a Rorschach test. Which could explain why most folks, hesitant to reveal a little too much of themselves, opt for the unobtrusive, safe, and simple choices, like plain cotton duck, classic terry cloth, or waffle-weave cotton. Although those utilitarian curtains get the job done, they're pretty much devoid of style or sass. And they represent a missed decorating opportunity—because nothing revamps the bathroom faster, cheaper, and with less effort than a shower curtain. Here are just a few of the solutions that will lift your bathroom out of the run-of-the-mill rut—or at least inspire new thinking. Don't see a pattern that suits your personality? Pay a seamstress to sew up a version using your favorite new or vintage fabric (it requires little more than a couple of hems and a dozen grommet holes). Either way, your shower curtain should do a heck of a lot more than just keep your floor from getting wet.

1. THE NEW SOPHISTICATE
Have an affinity for toile de Jouy but worry that it might come off as too stuffy and old-fashioned? Try a new take on the old French classic with a small, monochromatic, yet completely unexpected

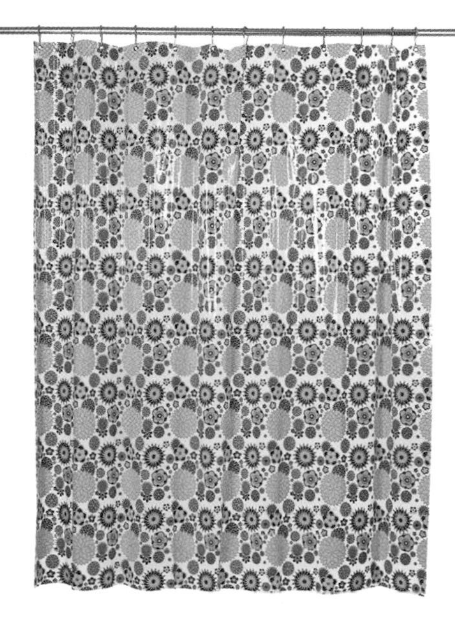

4.
THE FLOWER CHILD

5.
THE STYLE ICON

6.
THE CULTURE VULTURE

print, like these $10 palm trees from Pottery Barn.

2. THE ENVIRONMENTALIST
Stuck in the cement jungle? Need a little green to get you through? Find splendor in the photo-realist grass with Waterware's eternally verdant shower curtain. At around $30, it's a cheap alternative to an ecotour.

3. THE SOLID CITIZEN
Do you still think a flimsy white liner is a sufficient excuse for a shower curtain? Try this bright yellow number—or any vivid color—as a first step toward better self-expression. Ikea carries dirt cheap models like this heavy-duty plastic one (it's less than $5), but you can also look for striking solids at Bed Bath & Beyond, Target, and Kmart. Remember: the bolder, the better.

4. THE FLOWER CHILD
O.R.E.'s funky fusion of trippy wallpaper and bold Asian flowers looks like it was plucked straight from a Tokyo apartment, circa 1973. For less than $30, it's a small price to pay for such good vibrations.

5. THE STYLE ICON
If you're not the pattern type, go for a single centered image. Broken Spokes' crossover country chic number, a mere 30 bucks, is equally at home on the range or in the city.

6. THE CULTURE VULTURE
So you can't drop the big bucks for Damien Hirst's dotty pop piece, *Amonium Biborate.* That doesn't mean you can't appreciate what a deluge of dots does to your eyes. Decor Craft's Twister-inspired circles offer good clean fun—for less than $20.

5

Got an extra closet? A tiny alcove? You'll be surprised how easy it is to squeeze a desk into the most unlikely places. And you can do it even if money is tighter than space.

Home Office

Making room to work at home is often an afterthought or, for the space-starved among us, impossible to think about at all. But chances are, you don't need an elaborate setup–especially if you head out to an office every day. You can carve out a spot for a desk and chair in your bedroom, living room, or even your kitchen. Just make certain that your work area reflects the style of the surrounding room, like this windowed nook, opposite. For one busy publishing executive, a favorite table in a corner of her bedroom is both personal and professional. She painted it to blend in with her decor, and ingenious storage solutions keep it neat. If you work exclusively from home, you may want to commit more space to your endeavors, which is easier than you think. See page 150 to find out how a journalist sacrificed a closet but gained an efficient workstation. On page 146, a decorator transformed a spare bedroom into a design studio that's not only well equipped but also stylish and impressive enough to use for meetings with clients–thanks to "office" furnishings that came from everywhere but the office-supply store. After all, there's no reason you should have to write letters, pay bills, or face a deadline in deadening surroundings. Out in the open or tucked away, solely dedicated to work or serving other functions, your home office can be as comfortable and colorful–not to mention as clever and inexpensive–as every other room in your house.

The Convertible

THIS SMALL BEDROOM could have turned into a haphazard storage space, where questionable furniture and cast-off clothes languish in limbo. But interior designer Darren Ransdell had other plans for the extra room in his L.A. home. He made it stylish enough to compete with the rest of the apartment by painting the walls a serene green and then outfitting the room with everything but typical office furniture. Now he has a work space representative of his chic style, but one so efficient he can run his firm from it.

Outta sight: Some must-have supplies aren't easy on the eyes. So Darren Ransdell stowed ugly necessities—file cabinets, a fax machine, and a printer—in the closet.

Spare Room Redo

After six years of letting his extra bedroom lay dormant, Ransdell put his design skills to work and created an office that is both homey and hardworking. Here's what was behind his innovative thinking.

1 STEALTH STORAGE Converting a bedroom comes with a bonus: The closet makes a great supply pantry. Ransdell cleared out the rods and hooks, then outfitted the space with standard office organizers. What's with the drape? "I hung a cheap shower curtain from Bed Bath & Beyond in front of shelves jammed with ugly how-to books and other stuff." And he still had room to hide his printer and fax.

2 WONDROUS WALLS The designer is surrounded by a soothing shade of green (Dunn-Edwards flat latex in Lettuce Leaf) that is "also the color of money," he says with a laugh. Rather than hang bulletin boards, he displays an assortment of black-and-white photographs unified by black frames. The oversize clock (less than $50 at Ikea) continues the theme and keeps him running on time.

3 LOW-COST CARPET A fruitful rummage through the remnant pile at a local rug dealer yielded a generous piece of chocolate Berber and two odd-size plush mint strips. Ransdell had them bound for $300.

4 HEAVY METAL Slick white Naugahyde (cheaper than leather and easier to clean) revives a vintage Shaw-Walker office chair that Ransdell rescued from a secondhand shop for $200. He found the old military desk for $400 at Blackman Cruz, an eclectic L.A. furniture store.

POW-WOW
BURGERS
2394945 CF
02 01 94
QUEENS
71660934 D
2
4
3

Look for solutions in unexpected places. Kitchen and dining room furniture often offer up style and storage.

Design within reach: A glass-front flip-top kitchen cupboard, top, holds a variety of work items and flea market finds. Above: A hidden extension shelf under the TV is ideal for presentations.

Cabinet Positions

If you want to work amid a suite of standard office furniture, you might as well hang out in a corporate tower. But at home, think outside the cubicle. Why not adopt a kitchen table as a desk? Or use a chest of drawers as a file cabinet? In Ransdell's work space, Ikea, not Staples, proved to be the one-stop shop for his storage needs. Over his desk, he mounted a series of solid birch Värde kitchen cabinets (around $200 each), above. Right: Low storage, in the form of Pelto sideboards ($300 each) that were originally intended for the dining room, makes the most of unused space beneath the windows. The cabinets have smoothly sliding doors, so it's easy to hide clutter. The custom-built wall shelves are deep enough to accommodate a TV as well as design and art books. And the light wood prevents the pieces from seeming massive, striking a balance between the domestic and the disciplined.

PHOTOGRAPHY
ILLUSTRATION
MAYO CLINIC
ANDY GOLDSWORTHY
RM SCHINDLER

Office 98
Macintosh Edition
RECEIPTS
2003
HOLIDAY CARDS
dic·tion·ar·y
Cassell's French Dictionary
American Society of Magazine Editors
FEAR OF WINE
THE ART OF EATING
AVEDON THE SIXTIES
TWININGS
MEL RAMOS
Andy Warhol Prints
iMac

WHAT'S GIVING UP ONE SMALL CLOSET IF YOU GET A WHOLE ROOM OUT OF IT?

The Built-In

IMAGINE THE MESS a freelance journalist and mother of two can make without a proper place to work. Piles of books, newspapers, and notebooks, plus all that office equipment, can quickly make a hovel out of a home, especially one the size of the average Manhattan apartment. So, New York writer Liza Schoenfein and her editor husband put it all in a closet, which keeps her work organized and accessible but also out of sight. The best part: She can shut out work—and curious tiny hands—simply by closing the doors.

Hidden Treasure

A spare closet is something most New Yorkers wouldn't trade for anything, not even that other sought-after city commodity—a guaranteed parking spot. But for food writer Liza Schoenfein and her husband, Mark Jannot, deputy editor at *Popular Science* magazine, the conversion was a no-brainer. Rather than resort to old habits—in their previous apartment, they had a computer on a desk that rolled between the bedroom and kitchen—the couple committed the hallway walk-in, all 44 inches deep of it, to a home office. It was easy for Schoenfein to envision; the closet was stripped of its fixtures when they moved in. "When I first opened those double doors, I didn't see a closet, I saw a room," she says. And now, with a desk and shelves of white laminate custom-built by Creative Closets (for around $500), the couple can pack two professions worth of material into the compact space while still leaving room for style. Schoenfein and Jannot used blue Rust-Oleum to update plain black Staples file cabinets (around $70 each) and added a stylish swivel chair and bold striped rug (each around $20 at Ikea). The final personal touch comes from son Rex's artwork and two fabric-covered corkboards that hang on the inside of the doors. Just as important as adding charm to the space was making it easy to lock away. With Rex and his baby brother, Teddy, close at hand, the couple needed to ensure that their work didn't become child's play. Now all they have to do is close the doors to keep the kids at bay.

Open sesame: Beyond the unassuming double doors, top left, is evidence of a busy life. Clockwise from top right: Fabrics from Ikea and Hable Construction cover corkboards; a striped Ikea lamp gives the "room" a warm and homey glow; and a collage is held in place by ribbons and pins.

The Corner Office

A CHARMING Empire-style table follows Sarah Gray Miller wherever she goes—from the small town in Mississippi where she grew up, then on to college, and finally to New York City, where she tucked it into an unused corner of her bedroom. As editor-in-chief of *Budget Living,* she sits behind a big desk by day (and most nights, too), so a smaller (and considerably neater and more charming) home version, with its clever organizing solutions, is all she needs—perfect for paying bills, checking e-mail, and writing letters.

Quit fishing around for your stapler, scissors, and favorite pencil. A tackle box is perfectly designed to create order out of desktop chaos.

Tackling the Mess

Sometimes all you need is a small table and an overlooked nook to carve out a little office for yourself. Especially if most of your life is spent working at another bigger office. For Miller, the table, which has served as a desk since childhood, fits right into her small apartment. Painted at least as many times as it has been uprooted, the pristine white coat—it's Benjamin Moore's Decorator White—covers a lifetime's worth of doodles, coffee rings, and ink splotches. By painting it the same color as the wall, the desk fades into the corner without interrupting the tranquility of the room. The sleek glass chair, a take-home from a magazine photo shoot, practically disappears in its tight surroundings. Miller hung a series of landscape paintings, scored for $30 total at a thrift shop, directly over the desk to contrast with the modernity of the chair and iMac. With such a limited area, she had to find clever and attractive alternatives to file racks and pencil holders, which can quickly make a small area look disorderly. A vintage tackle box, an $8 junk shop find, makes the perfect supply "closet," keeping essentials organized and out of sight. Its slightly shabby exterior adds another layer of warmth to the pristine white space, too. A dish drainer, picked up at her favorite Harlem thrift shop for 50 cents, serves as a file holder and a catchall for thumbtacks, paper clips, and rubber bands. The clean, spare space is a welcome respite from a full-to-bursting inbox at her day job. And the well-traveled desk always reminds Miller that she's home.

LOVE LETTERS
INCOME TAX
Name
RENTAL PROPERTY
SHOE WISH LIST
CAR INSURANCE
BRIDGE CLUB
PARKING VIOLATION
PARTY DETAILS
iMac

Home Office Details

Sure, you could outfit your entire home office by shopping at the obvious supply stores, but it's unlikely to emerge as the most stimulating place to work. When it comes to furnishing the space, venture beyond the same old shelves and ordinary organizers to give it a shot of personality. If you love red, give the color full play on your wall with a mix of functional and decorative pieces like this corner, opposite. If a bookshelf holds your office necessities, as it does for one stylist, make it stand out like a fine piece of furniture by using reclaimed beams from an old building. Not into heavy construction? With just a couple of cans of paint, you can create a magnetic bulletin board in your favorite color. After all, it's your office, so don't let boring office-design dictates boss you around.

See the Little Picture

Your home office doesn't have to mimic a corporate corral to induce productivity. Give it a personal touch without putting that big family portrait on your desk by whipping up some photo magnets, above. Here's how: Head to the crafts store for small magnets and glass nuggets (or order them at Save-on-Crafts.com). Make photocopies of your favorite snapshots and trace the shape of a nugget onto each copy. Trim them a bit smaller than the outlines and hot-glue them to the back of the nuggets. Let dry, then hot-glue a small magnet onto the back of each picture. Left: A solid hit of red inspires Genifer Goodman to sit down in the tiny alcove she furnished with just a few well-chosen pieces. The Paul McCobb desk was a thrift shop steal at $400 (half of what they generally go for), and the bentwood chair was a gift from her partner. The cherry red Uten.Silo organizer, $200 at museum design stores, is "a bit steep," Goodman admits, "but it's less than two pairs of shoes, and it makes a great wall sculpture."

PROJECT: A GAME IDEA

If your Monopoly set is down to its last dollar and Miss Scarlet and Colonel Mustard are on the lam—with the lead pipe—don't despair. Instead of tossing the whole box in the trash, take the fun and games to a whole new level by turning the boards into display shelves. To make each shelf, just screw two four-inch L brackets into a wall and attach the board to the brackets using multipurpose cement. The Sorry! and Monopoly boards, right, were rescued from the trash, but if you're too proud to pick, you can buy new games at Toys "R" Us for less than $15. (Beneath the shelves: that most beloved of Ikea staples, Kassett CD boxes.) When choosing items for display, avoid anything heavy (the hot pink bowling ball stays in the closet) and take your cues from the game: We set astronauts atop our Star Trek board, above. But before you dismantle a mint-condition vintage set, remember that board games are the new lunch boxes; what was considered trash a few years ago is starting to fetch top dollar.

Cover your walls with clever castoffs to make display space that's anything but off-the-shelf.

Salvaged Stacks

You'd never know by looking at it that the bookshelf in Chip Cordelli's kitchen office was once a 30-foot center beam from a nineteenth-century building. That's because the inveterate scavenger, who discovered it in a collapsed building five blocks from his Brooklyn apartment, figured out a way to use the beautiful piece without having the square footage to accommodate it. Cordelli took his handsaw to the beam, cutting it up to fit the tiny space between the moldings around his front door and the entry to the living room. "It was so heavy, I had to cart the pieces home one at a time," he says. He mounted the wood to the wall with screws and L brackets. By extending the top shelf over the moldings, Cordelli gained additional display space. He used a steel brush to clean the wood but refrained from sealing it because "then it would be glossy and fancy." The dark wood is "very earthy, very beach house."

You work hard for your money, so don't waste it on a desk that won't pay you back. Here are six that are worth every cent.

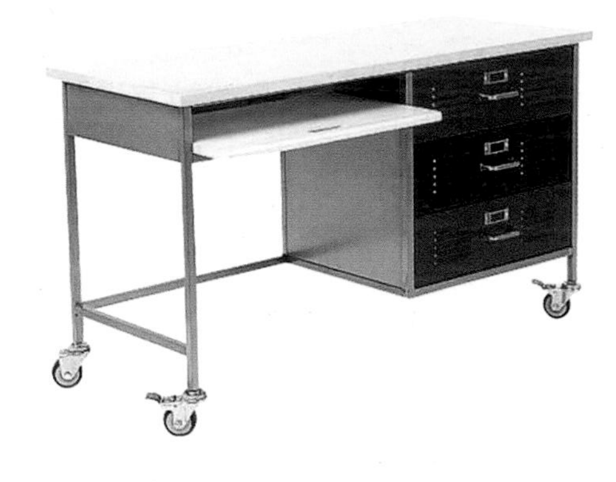

1. THE LIBRARY TABLE **2. THE SECRETARY** **3. THE RETRO ROLLER**

The Desk Set

There are as many desks out there as there are work habits. And the prices are just as varied. For a sleek place to park your computer, there's a solution for as little as $150, or you can spend up to $1,000 and hide your office behind closed doors.

1. THE LIBRARY TABLE
It's really a dining table, but you'll forgive our literary pretensions, especially when you learn that this solid birch beauty—at almost five and a half feet wide and just under three feet deep—will comfortably hold a hefty unabridged edition of Webster's and a PC and *still* leave room for lunching at your desk. At $300, it's affordable square footage from Ikea.

2. THE SECRETARY
The classic hallway catchall, the secretary's slim proportions make it a good fit for the space-starved. Crate and Barrel's is about three feet wide and less than one and a half feet deep, until you pull out the desktop, which gives you all the room you need for long nights of letter writing. At about $280, this secretary's a lot less expensive than the salaried kind.

3. THE RETRO ROLLER
It may look old school with the triplet of locker drawers complete with airflow vents, but the sturdy steel frame of PBteen's roll-about is fitted out with newfangled features. A pullout keyboard tray and casters make it flexible and movable. The desk frame will set you back around $450;

4. THE SUBCOMPACT

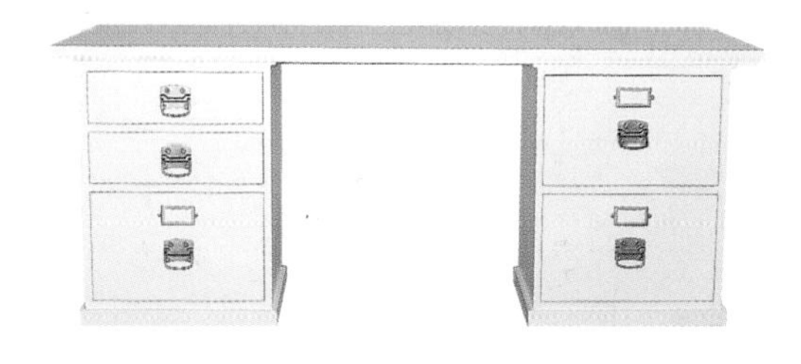

5. THE BARRISTER

6. THE WARDROBE

the drawers—which come in eight colors—are less than $50 each.

4. THE SUBCOMPACT
It looks a little like the lunar module, but Ikea's workstation is designed to bring you space right here on Earth. The mod unit is destined to end desk disarray by putting your computer and its accessories in their proper places. At approximately $150, it's one small—and cheap—step toward getting organized.

5. THE BARRISTER
Sit behind this generous desktop—it's 70 inches wide and 23 inches deep—and you'll have no problem keeping things orderly. It sits on top of two file cabinets and leaves you with lots of legroom. Pottery Barn's modular system goes for about $130 for the desktop and $200 for each cabinet.

6. THE WARDROBE
So much more than a desk, so much less of a space hog, a freestanding closet with shelves fitted specifically for a computer, keyboard, and supplies can open the door to the kind of organized work space you thought you'd never have at home. This media center from PBteen will cost ya—an even grand—but it solves a lot of storage problems: A fixed shelf holds your PC, a slide-out keyboard tray can be tucked away in a snap, and you can adjust one of the shelves. Cork-lined doors provide places to hang schedules, pictures, even dreaded bills. Close the doors and all the pressures of work will disappear.

Sure, the office-supply store
has everything you need.
But personalizing the
space is in your hands.

**PROJECT:
WASTE? NOT!**

It could be a commentary on the disposable nature of our society or an artsy statement about form and content. Happily, it's just a wastebasket easily constructed from a magazine. To make it, cut four same-size pages from your favorite mag for the sides and an additional page to whatever size you want the bottom to be. Prepare a mixture of one part matte-finish Mod Podge (available at most crafts stores) to two parts water. Using a plastic drop cloth as a work surface, brush three to five coats of Mod Podge onto each side of the magazine pages, allowing 15 minutes between coats. Each time you coat a page, place it on a clean part of the cloth to dry. Once all the pages have dried completely, use a paper punch to make holes a quarter inch from the edges of each page, at quarter-inch intervals. Then tie a knot at the end of a length of craft cord and loop it through the holes to sew your basket together, knotting the cord at the sides or the bottom as needed until you've finished connecting all the pieces and have created a matching border along the top.

PROJECT: RULES OF ATTRACTION

According to its label, Magically Magnetic Paint Additive will turn anything into a "magnetically attractive surface." Which is enough to make the perpetually single among us want to hop into a tub filled with the stuff. A much saner decision would be to bring a little romance to a barren wall. You can make a three-foot-by-four-foot inspiration board, like the one at right, with about a half gallon of the stuff (around $25), a quart of Kilz primer (less than $5), a quart of your favorite paint color (this one is Benjamin Moore Yellow Highlighter, about $14), and a roll of painter's tape (less than $3). Just mark off an area with painter's tape, stir together the additive and the primer, then roll on five coats of the mix. Allow an hour between the first four coats and a full day for the last to dry. The final step: two coats of latex paint in a flat finish. Let it set overnight, and in the morning, you may find yourself irresistibly drawn to your office.

Your bulletin board says a
lot about you. So why not
have it tell a good story?

Pretty as a Picture

Think of it as a frame for your favorite postcards, pages torn from magazines, and other paraphernalia that just begs to be displayed. Once you see the beauty—and utility—in pinning up your possessions artfully, you'll never look at a basic bulletin board the same way again. When decorating the bedroom for her partner's daughter, Lucy, Genifer Goodman transformed a standard corkboard into a stylish display, right—a rotating collection of prized invitations, souvenirs, and artwork. Pink (one of Lucy's favorite colors) always figures into the mix, keeping the arrangement from looking haphazard. Opposite: For Chip Cordelli, a piece of plywood serves as a humble vehicle for self-expression. He mounted it on a wall of his rental apartment to avoid doing any damage to the place (and ensuring the return of his deposit). The collage is a work-in-progress, according to the stylist, but as in the best home offices, the personal never takes a backseat to the work-related.

There's no easier way to expand your square footage than to make room for living outside.

Outdoors

You don't need fancy plants and pricey porch furniture—or even a porch–to create a space for yourself in the great outdoors. After all, why should your livable square footage end at the front or back door? Head out, and consider the possibilities. Mother Nature already supplies the decor and the views–and her color sense is always right on. When the sun is beating down and the breeze is in the trees, all you have to do is grab a comfortable chair, set it down in a cozy spot, and toast the day. Your outdoor retreat can be as casual as the place one happy couple made by putting an exterior wall to good use, opposite. They plunked down a makeshift table and a couple of sling chairs to settle in and sip their iced tea. (Follow their lead with one of the weather- and budget-friendly chaises shown on pages 182 and 183.) If you're after an outdoor room that's a bit more structured, there are still simple and inexpensive ways to get it. Add a rudimentary overhang to a shed to create a portico that will shelter you as you watch the rain or the stars. Or take inspiration from the landscape architect on page 170, who created a glorious garden behind his California rental cottage, putting down roots on land he doesn't even own. His trade secrets–portable and affordable decking, fencing, plants, even a D.I.Y. cinder block sofa–are all ready for the plucking. So turn the page and start harvesting.

HUMAN BODY
ANDY WARHOL

DECORATE YOUR FRONT PORCH AS IF IT WERE AN INTERIOR ROOM.

The Transformers

PERHAPS THE BIGGEST surprise about the Gothic mansion that Rob Pruitt and Jonathan Horowitz bought in the Catskills was that it came with a sunny wraparound porch. And despite their dark sense of humor, the duo knew just how to make the most of it. They gave the space all the comforts of an interior room but minimized the seriousness—and the expense—by using paint and witty plastic furniture. Most important, their quirky sensibility, even when exposed to daylight, remained intact.

The Power of Paint

Sure, Rob Pruitt and Jonathan Horowitz aren't the first people to paint a porch floor. Nor, for that matter, are they the only folks daring enough to choose a bold scarlet hue. But the genius here isn't the shocking color; rather it's the wide black band that sets off that sea of red and gives it the witty look of an interior carpet. The high-gloss enamel rug lays the groundwork for a decorating scheme that takes off from Victoriana, makes numerous stops in other decades, and lands in the '70s. "We wanted the place to have a period feel but didn't want something frozen in time," Pruitt explains. So he and Horowitz undercut the porch's late-1800s architecture by using a psychedelic fabric, which they found for just $25 on eBay, to upholster the iron love seat and chair. A $10 plastic urn from Kmart became a side table with the addition of a circular mirror on top. As for the red chairs lined up against the railing? They look like Thonet's mid-nineteenth-century bentwood Vienna cafe chairs, but they're actually $20 Ikea knockoffs, made of sturdy, weather-resistant plastic. The Swedish superstore also supplied the mod black plastic lounger, and it, too, cost only $20. In fact, Pruitt and Horowitz's sole splurge (if you can call it that) was the 75 bucks they spent on their coffee table, made from steamer trunk edges, at a Long Island, New York, design store. Finally, to give their porch the feel of a furnished parlor, the couple hung a piece of art (a vintage anatomy poster in a cheap frame) over the sofa and selected a single exotic plant: a somewhat spooky plastic orange specimen, whose frank fakery only adds to the fun.

An artist friend etched the ironic greeting on the front door. See page 136 to learn more about spelling out your own message on glass.

The Temp Job

RUSS CLETTA'S PROFESSION is making permanent changes to outdoor spaces, so imagine how the landscape architect felt about the dirt patch behind his rental cottage in Los Angeles's Venice Beach. If he ever lost his lease, he would lose his garden, too. Nevertheless, Cletta couldn't resist putting down roots. But before breaking ground, he struck a deal with his landlord: In exchange for gussying up the garden, Cletta's rent would never be raised. But just in case, when he's ready to move, his garden will be, too.

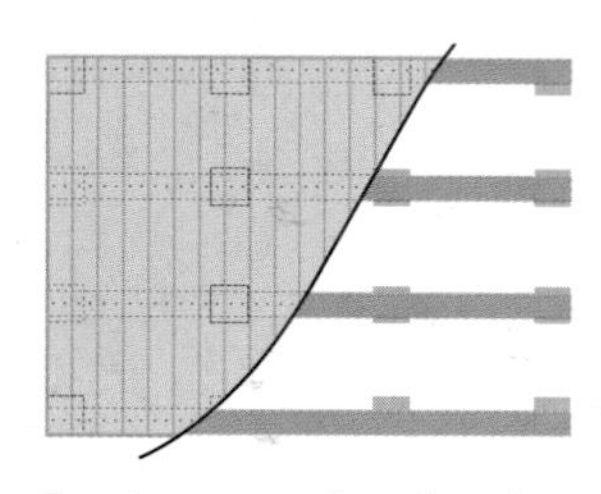

Four beams, each resting atop four concrete pavers, are all it takes to support Russ Cletta's deck, because it sits a mere six inches from the ground. The planks that constitute the deck's surface are screwed—not nailed—to the beams for easy dismantling later.

Good to Go

Despite his rental status, Cletta started in on the garden right away because it added much-needed entertaining space to his tiny 800-square-foot home. One of his budget-saving secrets is to make the most of what's already on hand—in this case, the back side of a neighbor's expensive translucent fence. Cletta highlighted it by installing a lower fence made of plywood scrap that he painted gray. He skipped grass and sprinklers and embraced budget-friendly and maintenance-free gravel instead. He dispersed plants—mostly castoffs from other gardeners—in portable pots. The end result: a permanent-looking landscape that can be pulled apart and moved to the next location.

PROJECT:
TOP DECK

In just a single afternoon, Cletta built a deck from pressure-treated Douglas fir planks and beams, which are screwed together and rest on concrete pavers so the deck can be easily dismantled. Sound like a house of cards? It isn't. The structure is stable because it hovers only six inches off the ground and is heavy enough to hold itself in place. The platform defines the outdoor dining room, furnished with a steel table (salvaged from a defunct office cafeteria) and junk-store chairs spray-painted silver. And you don't have to be a master builder to make a similar deck. Start by clearing a 10-foot-by-14-and-a-half-foot area and raking it flat. Next, lay down four equally spaced rows of four one-foot-square precast concrete pavers (about $12 total). Set them 40 inches apart for the length and 24 inches for the width. On top of these supports, lay four four-inch-by-six-inch pressure-treated Douglas fir beams, each 14 feet and two and a half inches long. At about $60 each, they don't come cheap, but they do offer supreme support. Then evenly place 31 two-inch-by-six-inch-by-10-foot pieces of pressure-treated Douglas fir planks (about $11 each) across the beams. Using two-and-a-half-inch deck screws ($5 per box), fasten each plank to the four beams. To keep the deck shipshape, seal out water and the elements with an opaque stain made by Cabot or Olympic (around $22 a gallon). The total cost of the materials should run less than $650—a small price to pay when you consider that your sturdy deck is nearly as portable as you are.

Turn your desolate backyard into a D.I.Y. dream garden with a few clever—and cost conscious—designs from a pro.

Low-Cost Custom

When Cletta, below, couldn't find stepping stones in sizes he liked, he made them himself for a song. He also assembled a lazy man's sofa from cinder blocks, plywood, foam, and outdoor fabric. Trust us: It's more comfortable than it sounds—and a heck of a lot cheaper than store-bought seating.

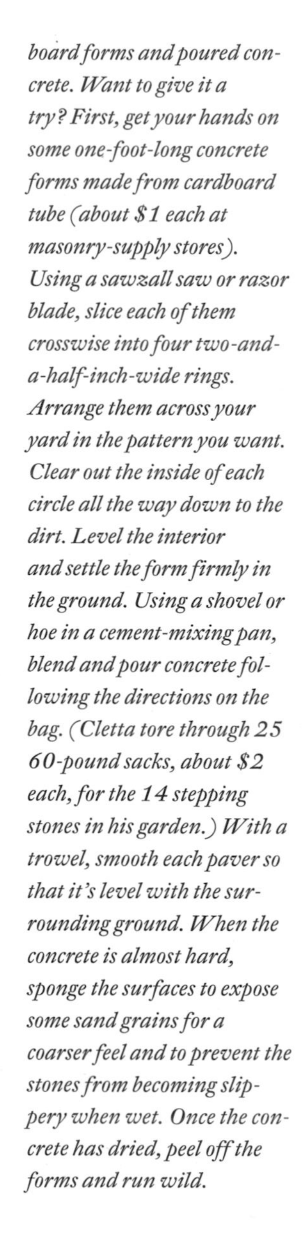

PROJECT: MAKE YOUR OWN PATH

First, Cletta evened out his backyard's terrain with a rake and covered the ground with two cubic yards of crushed three-quarter-inch gravel (the cheapest grade he could find) to create a low-maintenance, $30 outdoor floor. When he couldn't locate the perfect large round stepping stones for his path, he bypassed the building yard and made his own using cardboard forms and poured concrete. Want to give it a try? First, get your hands on some one-foot-long concrete forms made from cardboard tube (about $1 each at masonry-supply stores). Using a sawzall saw or razor blade, slice each of them crosswise into four two-and-a-half-inch-wide rings. Arrange them across your yard in the pattern you want. Clear out the inside of each circle all the way down to the dirt. Level the interior and settle the form firmly in the ground. Using a shovel or hoe in a cement-mixing pan, blend and pour concrete following the directions on the bag. (Cletta tore through 25 60-pound sacks, about $2 each, for the 14 stepping stones in his garden.) With a trowel, smooth each paver so that it's level with the surrounding ground. When the concrete is almost hard, sponge the surfaces to expose some sand grains for a coarser feel and to prevent the stones from becoming slippery when wet. Once the concrete has dried, peel off the forms and run wild.

PROJECT:

CONCRETE COMFORT

Kicking back is easy on an all-weather concrete couch. And so is making one. Find a spot that can lend a wall for back support. Level an eight-foot-by-two-foot area of ground and cover it with two inches of builder's sand for a stable base. (You'll need about two skips' worth—around $25 at most hardware stores.) Round up 32 concrete blocks (about $1 apiece) that measure eight inches by eight inches by 16 inches each. Firmly press down 16 blocks to fill the footprint and abut the wall, alternating short and long sides. Top with a second layer of 16, again alternating the pattern to help provide stability. To make the cushion, stack two three-quarter-inch-thick eight-foot-by-two-foot sheets of plywood (about $15 each) and top them with a piece of two-inch-thick high-density foam that's cut to the same dimensions (around $20 at upholstery stores). Wrap the stack in approximately two and a half yards of outdoor fabric (available through an upholsterer or awning company, or at OutdoorTextiles.com for about $14 a yard). Staple the fabric underneath the plywood and pile high with colorful pillows.

The Chimney Sweep

IT STANDS 18 FEET HIGH and towers over the tiny house. But the freestanding smokestack that architect Stephen Atkinson designed for his parents' retreat in rural Louisiana is as warm and inviting as any campfire. Although it wasn't easy for Stephen to convince his dad to spend almost a fifth of the house's entire budget on professional masonry work, the splurge wound up suiting both father and son. And it fits perfectly with the rest of the place—humble yet dramatic, warm and rustic but in a modern kind of way.

Tall Order

"We talked on the phone every night," architect Stephen Atkinson says. But that's to be expected when a son designs a house and the father builds it—especially if one collaborator is a perfectionist (Stephen) and the other is concerned about costs (John). The architect had cleverly specified that a deck should cut through the center of house, nearly doubling its square footage without doubling the cost. That way the interior could remain small without feeling cramped—especially in Louisiana, where the balmy climate allows the outdoor space to be usable nearly all year long. But what happens when temperatures do drop? Atkinson designed a tall chimney and outdoor fireplace that would stand sentry on the sleek deck. The splurge was hard-won—it ate up $8,000 of the $41,000 construction budget—and went up only after "some intense periods of negotiation," admits Stephen. Now, however, the Atkinsons can live as comfortably outside as they do in—even come December. Though the senior Atkinson built the house himself, his skills didn't extend to masonry. John's advice: "Know when to let go. Contract out tricky jobs. Masonry has a steep learning curve and, in some states, may require professional work to pass inspection."

Only in Louisiana, folks: On a November afternoon, Brenda, Stephen, and John Atkinson share a bottle of wine at a cypresswood dining table on their outdoor deck.

SOMETIMES A SIMPLE ROOF OVERHEAD IS ALL THE STRUCTURE YOU NEED.

The Swing Set

PAULETTE HOGGATT SITS IN one swing to take in the view of Lake St. John and in the other when she wants to look out at the cotton plantation in the distance. This little piece of real estate in Ferriday, Louisiana, has been transformed into a prized place for hanging out—literally—and a temple honoring the leisure life. Paulette's husband, Allen, used humble materials to build the portico off one wall of an old work shed, then installed twin gliders to provide the couple with a lifetime of views, one way or the other.

Tin Roof Rustic

Is that neglected shed in your backyard looking a bit beleaguered? You could tear it down—or turn it into a relaxing place to swing in the breeze, like Allen Hoggatt did. Using weather-resistant stock lumber, marine plywood, a few sheets of corrugated tin, and his own hands, Hoggatt attached the temple-front facade onto one of the outbuildings that dot the Louisiana lake property he shares with his wife, Paulette, below left. To frame the portico, he sunk supporting posts into the ground, built a skeleton for the roof, and covered the top in corrugated tin. Finally, he formed a pediment by attaching two triangular pieces of marine plywood underneath the front gable. As a finishing touch, he poured a concrete slab to serve as the floor, and just before it dried, he gave it a no-slip finish, using a push broom to create subtle grooves in the surface. By relying on inexpensive materials and leaving the wood bare, Hoggatt ensured that the add-on would increase the charm of the place, not ruin it. In fact, the pavilion looks as though it's been there forever. And this is one couple who appreciate age. They've proudly displayed many of the treasures that came with their house, which has been in Paulette Hoggatt's family since 1946. Among those mementos are the signs that hang on the shed's exterior and the old—now highly collectible—boat motor that sits like sculpture on the "fishing side of the building." The porch swing on the left also came with the house, while Allen built the one on the right himself, modeling it after a swing he loved as a child.

A trio of wheelbarrows rests against a boat on one side of the shack, above left. Above center: On the other side, a vintage Evinrude outboard motor serves as down-home sculpture. Above right: Paulette Hoggatt's childhood croquet set is still game.

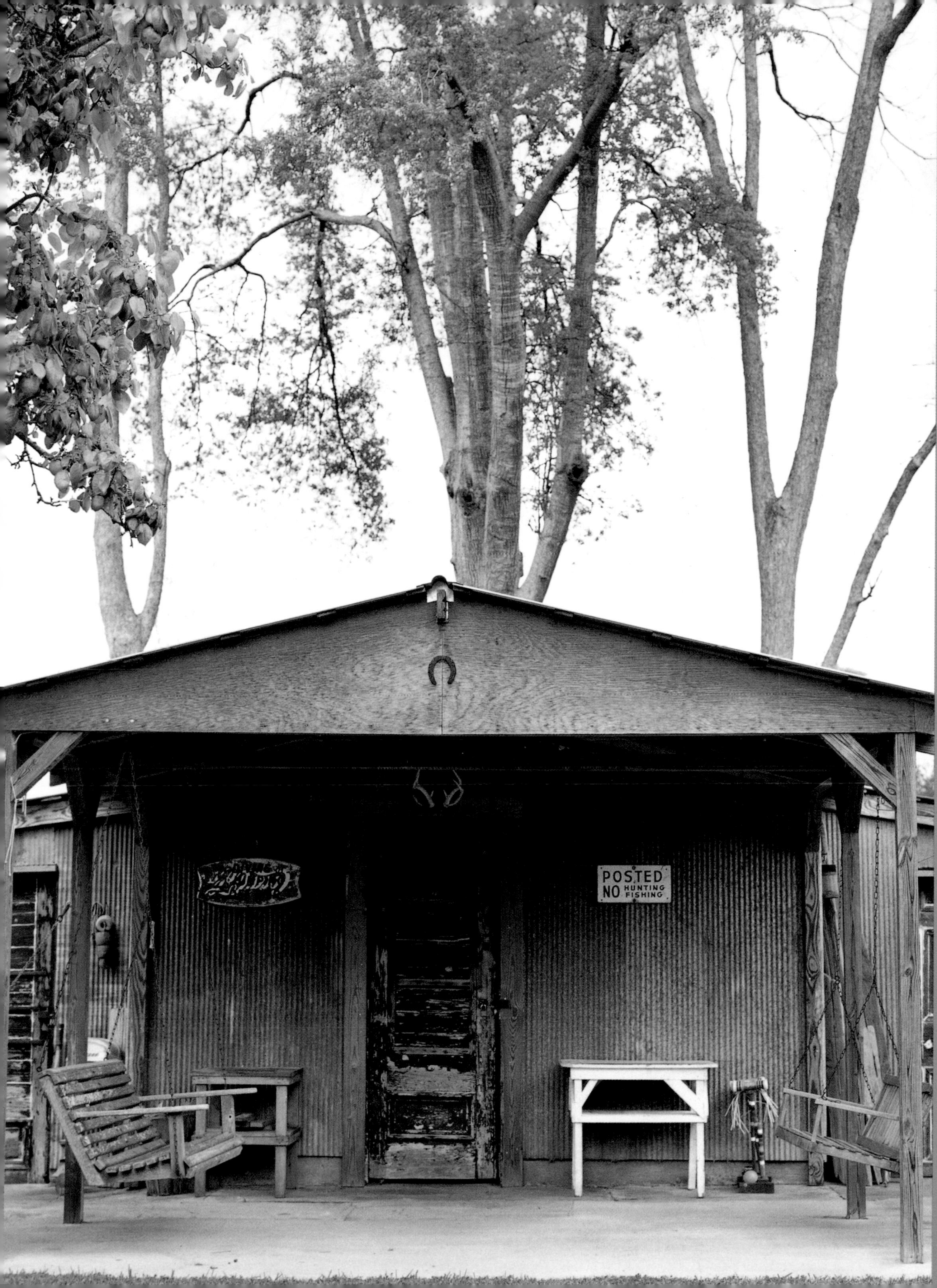
POSTED
NO HUNTING FISHING

Outdoor Details

Who would think that furnishing an outdoor room could be nearly as time-consuming—and expensive—as designing an indoor one? But the fact is, even if your floor is grass and your ceiling sky, you still need seating and a table or two to make the most of a warm afternoon. Fortunately, there is furniture to suit just about everyone's taste and budget—we've got proof on pages 182 and 183—and all of it is easily transported from the porch to the lawn and back again. Uninspired by standard-issue outdoor fabrics? Take a lesson from the designer, opposite, who made what works inside even more stylish on the outside. If you can't see spending big on fancy terra-cotta pots but don't want to resort to plastic, look at the clever options on pages 184 and 185. Herewith, some of the best ideas under the sun.

Weather Permitting

Sasha Emerson, left, with her husband, Larry Levin, and daughter, Isabel, paid only $10 for their butterfly chair, above. But she made it look like a million bucks—and practical for the outdoors—by having the metal frame powder-coated and the whimsical fabric laminated. Powder-coating creates a thicker finish than mere paint, and it's also completely weatherproof. The durable enamel lasts at least five years—even outside in the snow—but you'll need a pro to get the job done. The key to getting the most bang for your buck: Stick to a single color and have several pieces coated in one batch to avoid setup fees. Each setup usually costs less than $100; each chair runs between $25 and $50. Call your local autobody shop for recommendations. Emerson sends her favorite interior fabrics to David Gomez of L.A.'s Decorator's Laminating Service for the weatherproofing treatment. Ask a local interior designer if there's a fabric laminator in your area.

Here are two ways to change the ground you walk on. The tiny tiles take some time, but the pavers make a patio pronto.

Presto, Patio

Andy Hackman, owner of the tony L.A. furniture store California Living, sells reproductions of the mid-century table and bench set, right, for a whopping $1,750. His equally gorgeous modern patio, on the other hand, cost less than $50 to build. First, Hackman marked off a six-and-a-half-foot-by-11-foot area and leveled it by hand—hosing down the ground and smoothing it with two-by-fours. Then he laid 15 square 24-inch concrete pavers (about $2.50 each at building-supply stores) three inches apart to form a grid three pavers wide and five long. Hackman can't remember which contrasting ground covers he planted between his concrete slabs, but you can take a quick trip to the plant index at BHG.com to find an array of low growers suited to your climate.

Tale of the Tile

Ask Elaine Gemmell to divulge the story behind the mosaic at right and she begins, "My daddy's wife's sister's husband..." Whoa, sounds like one whopper of a complicated gothic yarn. The floor does indeed hail from the Deep South—it's installed on the back porch of the Gemmells' Louisiana lake house—but its genesis isn't the least bit convoluted. Back in 1972 Gemmell's mother discovered a box of mismatched leftover tiles in *her* brother-in-law's messy workshop, then convinced Elaine's father to install them in a random pattern—all in a single weekend. You can do the same using remnant tiles found on the Web (you could cover California with the selection on eBay alone) or by calling local contractors, who tend to keep unused scraps. When it comes to installation, we won't lie: It's tough, time-consuming work. For the best step-by-step directions, grab a copy of Home Depot's *Home Improvement 1-2-3* ($20) when you stop by to pick up grout. Then maybe one day your descendants will be spinning yarns about you.

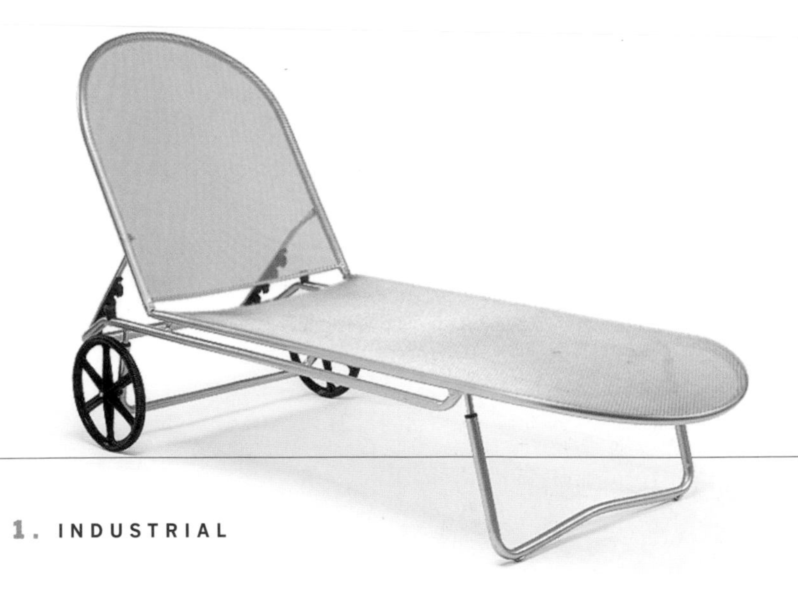

1. INDUSTRIAL

2. CLASSIC

3. WACKY WICKER

Lying Low

Who says that good design and comfort don't mix? It might be hard to argue the point if you're reclining on a La-Z-Boy, but if you're stretched out on one of these stylish chaises, your argument will stand up (even if you don't). Here are the six we like best for portability and price. Some are versions of those you dragged to the beach as a kid, others have a more exotic appeal. And not one will set you back more than $300. Now that should make even a tightwad relax.

1. INDUSTRIAL

Room & Board's silver lounger merges the sleek and modern with a slight retro feel. Its streamlined design is as friendly as an Airstream trailer and makes it easy to wheel around and follow the sun. At around $300, it's not cheap, but unlike your tan, its weather-resistant, powder-coated steel won't fade.

2. CLASSIC

You don't have to foot the bill for a berth on the *QE2* to enjoy lounging in a classic oceangoer. Pier One consistently offers updated versions

4. POOL COOL

5. BRITISH COLONIAL

6. RETRO

in an array of stripes and solids—and they're a titanic bargain at just under $70.

3. WACKY WICKER

Even those eminent Victorians would appreciate this modern take on their favorite porch fixture, the wicker chair. It's expensive for Ikea (though still less than $200), but not when you think of this sinuous rattan stunner as sculpture to sit on.

4. POOL COOL

Break out the foil reflector, the macramé bikini, and the Jacqueline Susann novels: This retro vinyl chaise—often available at Wal-Mart, Target, or Kmart—delivers '70s style at a groovy price (think less than $40).

5. BRITISH COLONIAL

With a pullout footrest and four reclining positions, Princess Jamaica Woodworks' fir-and-bamboo planter's chair, at around $150, adds exotic ambiance to even the most suburban of screened porches.

6. RETRO

Who hasn't parked a wet bathing suit on a beauty like this? It costs less than a movie and will last way beyond Labor Day, so it's the cheapest fun in town. This one's from DoItBest .com, but you can usually find these chairs at your local drugstore once summer begins.

There's no need to restrict your pot options to expensive imported terra-cotta or ugly plastic.

Contain Yourself

With an imaginative eye, any number of containers can suddenly become unexpected blooming opportunities. Take, for example, the shiny modern planter at right. Have you been putting off buying a large tree because of the high price of a stylish planter to go with it? Head to your local home center for the ultimate in industrial chic: a 30-gallon galvanized-steel trash can. This one cost $17 at Home Depot. If you're using it as a cachepot indoors, fill the bottom with a layer of pebbles and water to increase the humidity level. Outdoors, just drill or poke a few drainage holes in the bottom, plant your tree, and let the sun shine in. Opposite: The foreboding black tower in Rob Pruitt and Jonathan Horowitz's upstate New York yard is home to a full-fledged herb garden. But that's not what it was intended to hold. The vintage iron piece was a birdbath until the couple painted it with black marine-grade enamel and filled its tiers with potting soil and edible plants.

Resources

ABC CARPET & HOME
888 Broadway
New York, NY 10003
212-473-3000
www.abchome.com
This eight-floor Manhattan furniture store boasts the world's largest selection of high-end carpets, as well as a huge array of affordable remnants.

ASSOCIATED WEST IMPORTS
800-886-1916
www.associatedwestimports.com
An importer of Asian accessories (including a number of stylish lamps), Associated West doesn't sell directly to the public, but the company will point you to a retailer in your area.

B-4 IT WAS COOL
89 E. Houston St.
New York, NY 10012
212-219-0139
This shop, which specializes in twentieth-century antiques, offers a wide selection of anatomy posters.

BED BATH & BEYOND
800-462-3966
www.bedbathandbeyond.com
The megachain hawks everything from blenders to bath mats, ceiling fans to flatware.

BLACKMAN CRUZ
800 N. La Cienega Blvd.
Los Angeles, CA 90069
310-657-9228
www.blackmancruz.com
Proprietors Adam Blackman and David Cruz have culled an eclectic selection of twentieth-century vintage furniture.

BOCONCEPT.COM
This Danish company's stylish, sensibly priced modular furniture is now available stateside, thanks to nine U.S. locations.

BROKEN SPOKES MFG.
877-930-4369
www.brokenspokes-mfg.com
Former cattle hand Debbie Rottman sells cowpoke-themed housewares, including shower curtains, via the "cyber range."

CALIFORNIA LIVING LLC
601 N. La Brea Ave.
Los Angeles, CA 90036
323-930-2601
www.californialivingusa.com
Andy Hackman's sophisticated (if expensive) outdoor furniture shop carries original midcentury pieces and reproductions.

CRATE AND BARREL
800-967-6696
www.crateandbarrel.com
Stylish furniture, accessories, dishware, and more—all at truly palatable prices.

CREATIVE CLOSETS
212-496-2473
www.creativeclosets.info
Custom storage solutions that make the most of New Yorkers' meager square footage.

DESIGN WITHIN REACH
800-944-2233
www.dwr.com
With 16 showrooms, a mail-order catalog, and a bustling website, this San Francisco–based retailer is America's most popular source for high-end modern design.

DUNN-EDWARDS
888-337-2468
www.dunnedwards.com
Interior designer Darren Ransdell swears by this long-lasting paint, known for its soft Southwestern palette and sold primarily in the company's Arizona, California, Nevada, New Mexico, and Texas stores.

EBAY.COM
Want something vintage? Don't feel like scouring your local thrift shop or flea market? Start bidding already.

THE EVOLUTION STORE
120 Spring St.
New York, NY 10012
800-952-3195
www.theevolutionstore.com
This übergeeky natural-science store carries skulls, taxidermy, and a wide selection of vintage and new anatomy posters.

FUTURAMA
446 N. La Brea Ave.
Los Angeles, CA 90036
323-937-4522
www.futuramafurniture.net
Designer Sasha Emerson's favorite vintage furniture store stocks well-priced midcentury pieces by big-name and lesser-known designers.

GARNET HILL
800-870-3513
www.garnethill.com
The bedding offered through the company's catalog and website isn't necessarily the cheapest, but it is beautifully designed and made with natural fibers.

HABLE CONSTRUCTION
230 Elizabeth St.
New York, NY 10012
212-343-8555
www.hableconstruction.com
Sisters Katharine and Susan Hable hand-print their graphic textiles. Keep in mind, though, that buying their work constitutes a serious splurge. A throw pillow can set you back $200.

HELLER
212-685-4200
www.helleronline.com
Jonesing for the lightweight, weather-resistant, stackable ArcoBellini chair? This importer of Italian furnishings can point you to a store that carries it.

HOME DEPOT
800-553-3199
www.homedepot.com
If you can't find the materials for your project at this massive chain store, then you probably

shouldn't be building it.

IKEA
800-434-4532
www.ikea-usa.com
Smart, forward-thinking design at a truly unbeatable price. Avoid high delivery costs by shopping in person at one of the 18 stores nationwide.

KARTELL
866-854-8823
www.kartell.com
This prestigious modern furnishings company sells objects of contemporary lust, including a large number of Philippe Starck's designs, through a nationwide network of 15 dealers and proprietary stores.

KMART
866-562-7848
www.kmart.com
Our favorite reasons to hit the Big K: Krylon paints and the fabulous Martha Stewart Everyday collection.

KURT PETERSEN FURNITURE
847-692-5458
www.kpetersen.com
This virtual store stocks restaurant-supply wares, including vinyl diner furniture. Be sure to check out the deals in the GARAGE SALE section.

LINENS 'N THINGS
866-415-1333
www.lnt.com
One-stop shopping for all things fabric related.

LIZ'S ANTIQUE HARDWARE
453 S. La Brea Ave.
Los Angeles, CA 90036
323-939-4403
www.lahardware.com
With Liz's matching service, lone pieces of vintage hardware can meet their mate(s), thanks to an inventory of a million-plus knobs, pulls, and latches.

LOWE'S
800-445-6937
www.lowes.com
This home-improvement center prides itself on a great garden selection (plus, it'll special-order Summit stainless steel fridges).

MARTHA STEWART: THE CATALOG FOR LIVING
800-950-7130
www.marthastewart.com
It's not as cheap as her Kmart line, but Martha's premium catalog also has some truly premium merchandise.

MAURA DANIEL
3828 Clarington Ave.
Culver City, CA 90232
310-838-8844
www.mauradaniel.com
Maura and Daniel Cytrynowicz have taken floral to a whole new level with their 3-D silk-flower-studded lamp shades. Expensive but worth it.

O.R.E. ORIGINALS
800-367-2675
www.oreoriginals.com
The manufacturer behind some of our favorite shower curtains, O.R.E. is strictly wholesale, so call for a store near you.

PEARL RIVER MART
800-878-2446
www.pearlriver.com
These Chinatown emporiums—filled with everything from delicate paper lanterns to kitschy alarm clocks—have long been faves of style-savvy, cost-conscious Manhattanites. Now, thanks to a website, the

ARCHITECTS & DESIGNERS

Demi Adeniran
Fabrica LLC
New York, NY
212-587-6340

Stephen Atkinson
Studio Atkinson
Palo Alto, CA
650-321-6118
www.studioatkinson.com

Russ Cletta
Griffith & Cletta
Los Angeles, CA
310-399-4727

Rebecca Cole
Cole Creates
New York, NY
212-255-4797
www.colecreates.com

Christopher Coleman
Brooklyn, NY
718-222-8984

Chantal Dussouchaud
Atelier de Chantal
Beverly Hills, CA
310-271-0046
www.atelierdechantal.com

Sasha Emerson
Sasha Emerson Design Studio
Santa Monica, CA
310-230-9948

Charles de Lisle
Your Space Interiors
San Francisco, CA
415-565-6767

Henry Mitchell
Henry Mitchell
Interior Architecture
New York, NY
212-619-3320
www.hmia.net

Mark Naden
TODA
New York, NY
212-343-2414
www.toda.net

Darren Ransdell
www.darrenransdell.com

Lauri Ward
Use-What-You-Have
New York, NY
800-938-7348
www.redecorate.com

rest of the country can get in on the ancient Chinese secret.

PBTEEN
866-472-3001
www.pbteen.com
We jokingly refer to it as "puberty barn," but even those of legal age will appreciate this catalog's fun and financially sensitive inventory.

PIER ONE
800-245-4595
www.pier1.com
This nationwide chain may be known for the exotic look, but it's also a great source for basics like plain white napkins and solid-colored dinnerware.

POTTERY BARN
888-779-5176
www.potterybarn.com
Ground zero for classic pieces priced right.

PRINCESS JAMAICA WOODWORKS
800-757-0989
www.princessjamaica.com
Tim and Lynnae Molidor named their line of exotic outdoor furnishings after their favorite vacation spot.

PROPAGANDA
877-252-9366
www.propagandaonline.com
Everyday functional objects—say, a rubber drain stopper—that double as stylish, and extremely sly, works of art.

PURE DESIGN
780-483-5644
www.puredesignonline.com
Founded in 1994 by three industrial designers, this Canadian collective delivers sleek seating and shelving at decent, if not dirt cheap, prices.

REJUVENATION
888-401-1900
www.rejuvenation.com
These Seattle and Portland stores stock hundreds of repro lighting fixtures, most of which are also available on the Web.

RESTORATION HARDWARE
800-762-1005
www.restorationhardware.com
The furniture is more expensive than the offerings at Crate and Barrel and Pottery Barn, but this catalog and retail chain's retro-themed accessories set it apart from the pack.

ROOM & BOARD
800-486-6554
www.roomandboard.com
One of the widest selections of affordable upholstered furniture around. Stores are located in California, Colorado, Illinois, and Minnesota; elsewhere, order through the catalog.

ROOTS HOME
800-927-6687
www.roots-direct.com
This 30-year-old Toronto company's leather furnishings are available in the U.S. by phone order only.

SEARS
800-349-4358
www.sears.com
In addition to tools and electronics (and surprisingly fashionable clothing), the old standby also carries kitchen appliances from Frigidaire, KitchenAid, GE Profile, and Kenmore.

SMITH & HAWKEN
800-940-1170
www.smithandhawken.com
Even if your plants are plastic, check out these garden stores (or the company's catalog) for outdoor furniture stylish enough to be invited in.

TARGET
800-800-8800
www.target.com
In case you haven't already heard, this nationwide discount store has been reinvented as a gallery for marquee designers, such as Michael Graves, Todd Oldham, and Swell's Cynthia Rowley and Ilene Rosenzweig.

URBAN OUTFITTERS
800-282-2200
www.urbanoutfitters.com
These trendy clothing stores also stock a well-edited Apartment collection, with retro hanging lamps, shag rugs, and witty home accessories from Decor Craft.

WALLIES
800-255-2762
www.wallies.com
Most of these vinyl-coated wallpaper cutouts are a little too still-life-with-fruit for us, but their galloping horses are truly kickin' and easy to apply.

WAL-MART
800-925-6278
www.walmart.com
You know this superchain has the lowest prices, but look a bit harder and you'll find high style, too.

WATERWAREINC.COM
This Long Island, New York, purveyor has made a splash with its line of photo-realist shower curtains.

WEST ELM
75 Front St.
Brooklyn, NY 11201
866-428-6468
www.westelm.com
Pottery Barn's hipper-than-thou cousin has developed a cult following for its spare, Zen furniture sold at an equally minimal cost. Wanna see the wares in person? The sleek catalog was recently joined by a flagship store in Brooklyn.

YAYODESIGNS.COM
This cutting-edge artists' collective creates witty home accessories, including a series of plastic lamps that only animal or kitsch fans could love.

Credits

PHOTOGRAPHS

Cedric Angeles
pages 53, 59.

André Baranowski
pages 17, 45 (bottom), 50, 55, 80 (top), 110, 112, 159 (center), 160–161.

Marc Berenson
pages 60 (left), 115 (right).

Bo Concept, courtesy of
page 39 (bottom).

Crate and Barrel, courtesy of
page 158 (center).

Roger Davies
pages 18, 49 (top), 52, 54, 64–65, 111 (bottom), 130 (right), 131, 150–151, 168–169, 184.

John Dolan
pages 13, 93.

Amy Eckert
pages 10–11, 24–25, 119, 122–123, 128–129, 138, 157, 162.

Laura Fenton
page 41 (top).

Jim Franco
pages 14, 15, 16 (top left and top right), 36–37, 62, 63 (right), 86, 98 (right), 99–101, 125.

Steven Freeman
pages 41 (bottom), 115 (left).

Frigidaire, courtesy of
page 63 (center).

Christopher Gallo
pages 45 (top), 114 (right), 124, 137, 166, 185.

Gregory Garry
page 113.

General Electric, courtesy of
page 63 (left).

Christopher Hirsheimer
pages 4, 136, 152–153.

Ikea, courtesy of
pages 38 (top), 39 (top), 158 (left), 159 (left).

Deborah Jaffe
pages 7, 20–21, 56–57, 66–67, 77 (bottom), 109 (top), 117, 155 (bottom), 163, 171–173.

Frances Janisch
page 111 (top).

Eric Anthony Johnson
pages 140–141.

Michael Kraus
pages 9, 12, 16 (bottom center), 58, 92, 98 (left).

Francesco Lagnese
pages 39 (middle), 114 (left).

Jon Lam/Detour Photo
pages 42–43, 78–79, 115 (center), 144, 155 (top), 156, 182–183.

Winnie Lee
pages 81, 135 (top).

Maura Daniel, courtesy of
page 47 (right).

Ericka McConnell
pages 90–91, 118, 120, 167, 176–177, 190.

Joshua McHugh
pages 31, 32 (right), 33 (bottom).

William Meppem
pages 22–23, 60 (right), 77 (top), 83, 104–105, 145, 179.

Julie Mihaly
pages 51, 181.

Lynne Palazzi
pages 30 (bottom), 32 (left), 33 (top).

Joshua Paul
pages 40, 106–107, 139, 142–143, 164–165, 174–175, 180.

PBteen, courtesy of
pages 158 (right), 159 (right).

Katie Priester
page 80 (bottom).

Melissa Punch
pages 19, 46, 47 (left and center), 85, 130 (left).

Pure Design, courtesy of
page 114 (center).

Laura Resen
pages 116, 121.

Room & Board, courtesy of
page 38 (bottom).

Roots Home, courtesy of
page 38 (middle).

Susan Seubert
pages 8, 96–97, 188.

Tim Street-Porter
pages 35, 84, 87, 94–95, 132–133.

Ann Summa
pages 26–28, 49 (bottom), 68–75, 88–89, 102–103, 109 (bottom), 126–127, 135 (bottom), 146–149.

ILLUSTRATIONS

Ariel Asken
pages 28–29.

Don Bishop
page 170.

COVER PHOTOGRAPHS

Michael Kraus
front right, back bottom.

William Meppem
front left.

Ann Summa
back top.

Index

SUBSCRIPTION OFFER

Get BUDGET LIVING Magazine on the cheap!

Subscribe now for the introductory price of $14.95 for a year's worth (six issues) of ideas on how to Spend Smart and Live Rich. To subscribe, visit www.BudgetLivingMedia.com or call toll-free 1-800-588-1644. Ask about our special gift offer.

Additional postage: $10, Canada; $15, other foreign countries. Payable in U.S. funds only. Please allow 6–8 weeks for delivery of your first issue.

Look for BUDGET LIVING's next book Party Central in bookstores October 2004.